Financial Recovery in a Fragile World

How to Survive and Thrive in Uncertain Times

Al Emid and Robert Ironside
with Evelyn Jacks

KNOWLEDGE BUREAU
NEWSBOOKS

WINNIPEG, MANITOBA, CANADA

Al Emid and Robert Ironside with Evelyn Jacks

FINANCIAL RECOVERY IN A FRAGILE WORLD
How to survive and thrive in uncertain times

Printed and bound in Canada

Library and Archives Canada Cataloguing in Publication

Emid, Al, 1946-
    Financial recovery in a fragile world: how to survive and thrive in
uncertain times / Al Emid, Robert Ironside; with Evelyn Jacks.

ISBN 978-1-897526-76-7

1. Finance, Personal. I. Ironside, Robert, 1951- II. Jacks, Evelyn, 1955- III. Title.

HG179.E55 2011   332.024   C2011-906615-7

Publisher:
Knowledge Bureau, Inc.
187 St. Mary's Road, Winnipeg, Manitoba Canada R2H 1J2
204-953-4769 Email: reception@knowledgebureau.com

Publisher: Evelyn Jacks
Editor: Tessa Wilmott
Cover and Page Design: Sharon Jones

*To everyone who listens to today's financial news,
tries to connect the news to his or her financial affairs
and is looking for a roadmap through the chaos.*

— Al Emid

*To my family, friends and students who motivate
me always.*

— Robert Ironside

*The love and support of my family and colleagues, the
kindness of my friends, and the important work done
by the dedicated tax and financial professionals who
share knowledge with us at the Knowledge Bureau,
inspire me to share my passion and experience.
This book is dedicated to all of you.*

— Evelyn Jacks

Table of Contents

Acknowledgements

I would like to thank the individuals who took valuable time from their crowded schedules to help me make sense of a confusing and volatile world. They co-operated both in lengthy interviews and in what may have seemed like endless back-checking but understood the importance of both activities. To the extent that this book helps you, the reader, I owe it to them. I would also like to thank Florida- and New York-based researcher-consultant Steve Spector who never flinched, no matter what I asked of him.

I would also like to thank readers who, looking for answers in this confusing world, give our concepts and strategies fair consideration. We hope that they help you to make sense of the maelstrom of our times.

Al Emid
Toronto
November 2011

Writing a book such as this one is somewhat akin to writing in the sand as the tide comes in. Whatever you say, it will be overtaken.

The world in 2011 was rife with turbulence — and that uncertainty hasn't ended. Will the Eurozone remain intact or will it be shattered by the problems of the periphery? Will the U.S. overcome its political inertia and deal with its debt problems? Will Japan shake off twenty years of subpar growth before its debt problems overtake it? Finally, will China be able to transform its economy from export juggernaut to balancing force within the world's economy? Nobody knows the answers to these and many other questions but, as investors, we have no choice but to move forward, making the best choices we can with the information we have. It is my hope that this book will provide some sense of direction in a fragile world where there is none.

This book is a collaborative effort. The initial concept grew out of several discussions with Evelyn Jacks, founder of the Knowledge Bureau and author extraordinaire, and Al Emid, a financial journalist with years of experience. It evolved as we were writing. In a challenging and fascinating way, events moved faster than we anticipated.

Writing any book demands sacrifices and this one is no exception. I want to thank my students for their constant motivation and for their patience as I tried to bring this to a conclusion. I want to thank Stacy Yao for her excellent research assistance. Had I known earlier how good she is, it would be a better book. Finally, I want to thank my wife and family for their forbearance in allowing me to spend time on "the book" when I should have been with them.

Robert Ironside
Vancouver
November 2011

New grass always sprouts from underneath the rubble left by a storm. Recovery is about the experience of healing and the great joy of returning to health. It's also about the cherished new relationships we make no matter how difficult the journey. Things may be different after the storm, but not necessarily worse.

I would like to thank my co-authors, who took on the difficult challenge of writing a book about financial recovery in a fragile world in the midst of very turbulent times. Also, special thanks to our editor, Tessa Wilmott, who took on the equally difficult challenge of bringing three voices together. Her wisdom, skill and patience helped us accomplish what we set out to do: write a book that provides knowledge, insights and guidance to our readers. Finally, I would like to thank the book's designer, Sharon Jones, whose skill and perseverance brought our words alive on these pages.

It's also important to recognize the dedication and skill of the thousands of financial and tax professionals who work with their clients to get the financial results those clients need to survive and thrive in a volatile and shifting environment. They do important work, which includes the challenge of keeping their clients on plan. In particular, I have deep admiration for those who invest in their own professional development to do things differently, because that's the right thing to do in these times.

As always, a very special thank you to our staff at the Knowledge Bureau for their ongoing support.

Evelyn Jacks
Winnipeg
November 2011

Foreword

HOW DO YOU RECOVER FINANCIALLY in this fragile world? The economic circumstances are unprecedented; we have never before experienced a synchronous global financial malaise of this magnitude. Our financial landscape has been forever altered.

On the horizon, however, beyond the financial storm, there is a bright future, a safe haven where you can find financial security. The goal of *Financial Recovery in a Fragile World* is to help you assess your environment and chart your course so you can navigate successfully into that harbour.

The authors believe that if you can identify the "fingers of instability" within your own financial affairs, you will be able to reduce financial vulnerability, avoid further financial disaster and rebuild your real wealth. You may need to work on your investment approach and your financial relationships with your family and advisory teams; you may need to make a commitment to change. But all of these can be accomplished if you follow the course set by *Financial Recovery in a Fragile World*.

There are, indeed, many routes to financial recovery. For some, financial recovery is about disaster management. These are the individuals who did not foresee the approaching storm and had no disaster recovery plan; they, in fact, may have sleepwalked through the crisis hoping for a miracle, hoping someone would save them. Financially weakened by the force of the gale, their choices for the future are few. If that's you, this book will help you recognize what you can do to initiate your financial recovery and brighten your outlook for the future.

For others, financial recovery is a process of rebuilding. They may have had a financial fortress from which to weather this economic storm and they understand repairing damage to personal and family net worth is a good start. They know what needs to be done but they may not have a framework for achieving those goals. If that is you, *Financial Recovery in a Fragile World* will help you turn challenges into opportunities.

But, in a vulnerable global economy, all decisions are challenges. It will probably take several years for the world economy to repair itself and several decades to recoup the losses incurred. That's why the authors recommend an intergenerational approach to wealth management. The economic power of the family unit can strengthen and extend the opportunity for each individual's finances to recover. Recovery is most effective if we can preserve purchasing power.

Families have the opportunity today to leverage their most precious assets — time and money — to increase their net worth. They can fill the holes left by high fees, unpredictable markets and even inappropriate financial behaviour with real and immediate savings from tax-savvy money management and family income splitting. We hope to help you understand how to invest with caution as stability returns to the marketplace. Tax efficiency is a large part of this effort. It can help you hedge against inflation and future interest rate hikes. It's the most important tool in preserving wealth now and later when assets are transferred within the family.

We are certain there is a golden future ahead. Those who recover with strength will be in the best position to seize the opportunities the future brings. What does that mean to you from both a macro and a micro perspective? We are going to provide insights and explanations in the hopes that we can provoke good thought about how to begin to recover financially in a fragile world.

Al Emid
Evelyn Jacks
Robert Ironside

PART 1

How Fragile is our Financial World?

CHAPTER 1

Our Global Economy

MONDAY, SEPTEMBER 15, 2008, was a game changer. When, in the wee hours of that morning, Lehman Brothers Holdings Inc. filed for Chapter 11 bankruptcy protection — becoming the largest bankruptcy in U.S. history — it threw not just the United States but the world into turmoil. It marked the beginning of a whole new ball game globally, one in which the rules are uncertain, the players tenuous and the playing field volatile. Since then, careening stock markets and vanishing liquidity, collapsing businesses and government bailouts, rising unemployment and shrinking personal wealth, government austerity and citizen protests have become the hallmarks of our day-to-day life.

Welcome to our fragile world. In our turbulent economy, financial recovery does not mean picking up where we left off in 2008, nor does building personal wealth mean simply riding the latest wave of economic growth. In our fragile economy, financial recovery requires strategic thinking and careful planning; our personal recovery requires discipline, personal effort and commitment.

That's a tall order for most families — but the goal of this book is to help you to do just that. This book will help you examine our fragile world and understand the forces at play, so that you can make better decisions about your family's finances. None of us can predict the future but a better understanding of the past can inform the present. So, too, can the advice and observations of trained professionals.

With that in mind, this book will also introduce you to the principles of "Real Wealth Management.™"[1] Apply these principles and you can successfully navigate the prolonged period of sluggish growth and financial volatility that will characterize the next few years. *Financial Recovery in a Fragile World* will provide the tools you need so that you can think strategically, plan carefully and build real, sustainable wealth.

A World Awash in Debt

So, how can the bankruptcy of one American company cause such global havoc? In the fall of 2008, Lehman Brothers was the fourth largest investment bank in the United States with assets of US$639 billion but bank debt of US$613 billion and bond debt of US$155 billion. Befitting an investment bank of its status, it had connections all over the world. In a global economy, where money has no borders, Lehman Brothers had done deals and distributed product throughout the developed world. It had assembled buckets of securities including mortgages and credit card debt, many of questionable quality, and sold these derivative products globally, as had its competitors. As a result, when financially burdened mortgage holders defaulted in the southern U.S., the reverberations were felt as far away as Japan and Norway.

But the default of Lehman Brothers alone could not have triggered a global meltdown if the economic well-being of the "growth decades" had not been built on the shifting foundation of ballooning debt. For the past forty years, both governments and consumers have accumulated debt. With interest rates low and credit cheap and easily available, consumers used debt to support affluent lifestyles while governments fuelled economic growth with debt-financed spending. Neither was sustainable. Then, when the global economy shattered in 2008, governments everywhere had no choice but to fill the void left by overextended consumers confronting their economic mortality and shore up faltering economies with more spending. They dug themselves deeper into debt.

> *The fate of Lehman Brothers was but the final grain of sand that lead to a global economic landslide.*

But this is not intended to be a book that delves into the causes of the financial crisis that began in 2008; many excellent books have already been

---

[1] Real Wealth Management is a discipline and a framework for building sustainable family wealth over time, developed by the Knowledge Bureau, a national Canadian educational institute. For more information visit www.knowledgebureau.com.

written on the topic.[2] Instead, *Financial Recovery in a Fragile World* will look at the lessons of the recent past and assess their impact on the future, so you can prepare yourself — and protect your assets — for the future.

Black Swans

If it is so important to protect and prepare ourselves, both as governments and individuals, why weren't we better prepared for the events of 2008 and those that followed? Did the meltdown really come out of nowhere — or did it just seem that way?

Many of us — including economists — had our heads stuck in the sand, happy in our worlds, refusing to see the signs of the impending crisis. Those market watchers who tried to sound the alarm were often derided as cranks or "permabears," those habitually bearish individuals who see impending disaster even when the world is rosy. In fact, some researchers blame the economics profession itself; they maintain economists may have become complacent, believing that they had mastered the intricacies of the business cycle and that major recessions were largely a phenomenon of the past, or at the very least relegated to less developed and less sophisticated markets than the United States.[3]

Or was it something else entirely? Was it what author Nassim Nicholas Taleb would describe as a "black swan"? In his 2007 book, *The Black Swan: The Impact of the Highly Improbable*, Taleb describes a black swan event as having the following three attributes:

> First, it is an outlier, as it lies outside the realm of regular expec-
> tations, because nothing in the past can convincingly point to its
> possibility. Second, it carries an extreme impact. Third, in spite of
> its outlier status, human nature makes us concoct explanations for
> its occurrence after the fact, making it explainable and predictable.[4]

---

[2] The official version of the causes, *The Financial Crises Inquiry Report: Final Report of the National Commission on the Causes of the Financial and Economic Crises in the United States* (January 2011) can be found at http://cybercemetery.unt.edu/archive/fcic/20110310173738/http://www.fcic.gov/report/.

[3] There have been several excellent articles published on the failure of the economics profession to predict the crash of 2008 or even to admit that such a thing was possible. For example, see David Colander, Michael Goldberg, Armin Haas, Katarina Juselius, Alan Kirman, Thomas Lux and Brigitte Sloth, "The Financial Crisis and the Systemic Failure of the Economics Profession," *Critical Review* 21, nos. 2-3 (2009), pp. 249-267.

[4] Nassim Nicholas Taleb, *The Black Swan: The Impact of the Highly Improbable* (New York: Random House, 2007).

Taleb believes that much of history is a result of black swan events that were unpredictable, even inconceivable, prior to their occurrence, such as the terrorist attacks of September 11, 2001, or the 2011 earthquake off the coast of Japan. If we had known, we would have been prepared for those events.

> *It isn't what we know that hurts us, but what we don't know or failed to anticipate.*

If what Taleb says is true — and there is evidence to support him — we cannot hope to predict the next black swan event, nor can we accurately predict the behaviour of financial markets. That means you have to be prepared for the unexpected and the unpredictable.

The task of this book is to help you insulate your investment portfolio from the forces that will come to bear in the next few years. By understanding the nature and timing of life events that require serious decisions, then following a strategic process with a team of astute advisors, you can make those crucial decisions with confidence. That's important, because times of great volatility are those in which your wealth will sustain the most damage. But these times will also bring with them important opportunities.

What Can You Do to Recover?

- You can take your first step to recovery by opening your mind to the insights and practical advice contained in *Financial Recovery in a Fragile World*. In three parts this book will explore:
  - the global events of the recent past that have forged the challenges of today;
  - the lessons of today that we can apply to tomorrow's unknowns; and,
  - the methods by which we can insulate our wealth and make it grow.

CHAPTER 2

The Big Risk:
The House That Debt Built

THE EVENTS OF THE PAST FEW YEARS have shattered any illusions the Western World may have had about a "short-lived" crisis and an easy return to economic stability. Take the summer of 2011, when U.S. government antics over the raising of that country's debt ceiling tipped our delicate balance and fear once again sent markets plummeting. Take the riots in Greece that so graphically illustrated the personal cost of government austerity.

No sooner do we think we are on the road to recovery, then wham! we hit a bump that sends the global economy careening off course. And, by all accounts, we can expect many more potholes on the road to recovery, not to mention the occasional hairpin turn. There is a growing recognition that decades of easy credit, low inflation and unchecked spending — both by governments and individuals — took us to the brink. Now a decade of fiscal rebalancing is needed as people and governments get their financial houses in order. "Prolonged" is the descriptor of the day.

That is truly unsettling because this comes at a time when governments have greater demands on their resources than ever. That demographic bulge, the baby boomers, is reaching retirement age in several Western nations. The boomers will need pensions and, probably, health care. Governments pay for pension plans (most of which are unfunded or "pay as you go"), social programs and health care, just for starters. According to the Organization for Economic Cooperation and Development (OECD), in most member countries in 2008 "social protection" was the largest category of expenses, on average representing 34% of total expenditures; spending on health accounted for another 14.7%.[1]

Unfortunately, governments have a small and very finite number of ways they can deal with excessive levels of debt. They can reduce spending, increase revenue (that is, raise taxes), exercise their right to default on their obligations or inflate their way out of the problem. None of these options are good for investors. This decade of fiscal rebalancing and restraint couldn't come at a worse time.

Financial recovery in today's fragile economy is, indeed, elusive.

Bumps in the Road

So, how big an issue is debt? Is it big enough to derail a recovery completely? That is certainly a risk we have to consider as we prepare ourselves and our personal wealth for what lies ahead.

According to the OECD, the net central government debt of its thirty-four member countries reached US$22.2 trillion in 2010.[2] Of that, more than 40% or US$9 trillion belonged to the U.S. That compares to 1997 when total net debt for OECD countries was US$11.6 trillion; the U.S. portion of that was US$3.8 trillion or slightly less than 33%. To put these numbers in perspective, net government debt in OECD countries grew at an average rate of 5% a year during that fourteen-year period.

That would have been sustainable if the countries' economies had been growing at the same rate. But, sadly, that wasn't the case. Using gross domestic product (GDP) as a measure of what a country produces and a proxy for economic growth, the average increase in GDP for all OECD members during that same fourteen-year period was 2%,[3] creating a significant gap.

Why is it significant? If a country's debt grows at the same rate as its GDP, its ability to pay interest on that debt remains approximately constant, as long as interest rates stay constant. But when debt grows significantly faster than GDP, the country is on a dangerous path. Both debt and the cost of servicing that debt become larger than what the country's economy produces. When the debt relative to GDP reaches a certain size, those who are buying that country's bonds perceive greater risk and demand a higher

---

[1] Organization for Economic Cooperation and Development, *Government at a Glance 2011* (Paris, 2011).

[2] Organization for Economic Cooperation and Development "StatExtracts" online database, total central government debt, found at http://stats.oecd.org, accessed 25 October 2011.

[3] Organization for Economic Cooperation and Development, Economic outlook 89 database, found at:http://www.oecd.org/document/61/0,3746,en_2649_34573_2483901_1_1_1_1,00. html, accessed 6 November 2011.

premium to hold the bond debt, pushing the cost of servicing the debt even higher. That, in turn, forces the debt to grow even faster. When the time of reckoning comes and governments have to pay down debt, as they do now, growth in GDP is severely constrained. It becomes a vicious circle.

The OECD report, *Government at a Glance 2011*, echoes these concerns. Debt levels, it says, have increased sharply because GDPs in its member countries have not grown enough to offset heavy spending on stimulus measures, social transfers and bailing out sinking financial institutions. "As a result," the OECD report says, "the average OECD member country's public debt rose to 74% in 2010 from 57% of GDP in 2007."[4]

Put another way: "In the pre-crisis period between 2000 and 2007, OECD member countries decreased their share of government spending on average by 0.6 percentage points of GDP. However, after the start of the crisis, the share of government spending increased by 4.9 percentage points across the OECD during 2007-09."[5] That means, in that three-year period, the average net debt in the OECD countries grew by about 11% a year.

The irony is that in response to a financial crisis that was fostered by debt and fuelled by cheap credit, countries have tried to spend their way out of the economic downturn with stimulus packages and costly bailouts. The result has been rapidly increasing levels of debt relative to GDP across the entire developed world.

The key point to remember is that debt fuels growth in an economy as long as it is growing relative to GDP, but once that debt reaches a certain level, debt becomes a drag on the ability of the country to grow. Increasing amounts of the government's scarce resources have to be dedicated to debt-service costs, rather than funding programs and services that make a difference in people's lives.

Good Debt or Bad Debt?

Is there such a thing as good debt? Or, is all debt bad?

The Bank for International Settlements (BIS) released an important paper in September 2011 that attempts to answer that question. The paper's authors looked at government, non-financial corporate and household debt in eighteen OECD countries from 1980 to 2010. They determined that *all debt becomes a drag on growth once it reaches a certain percentage of GDP.*

---

[4] Organization for Economic Cooperation and Development, *Government at a Glance 2011* (Paris, 2011), p. 82.

[5] Ibid., summary.

"At moderate levels, debt improves welfare and enhances growth," they say. "But high levels can be damaging."[6]

When does debt cross over from good to bad? To quote the BIS report again: "For government debt, the threshold is around 85% of GDP. Our examination of other types of debt yields similar conclusions. When corporate debt goes beyond 90% of GDP, it becomes a drag on growth. And for household debt, we report a threshold around 85% of GDP, although the impact is very imprecisely estimated."

Once government debt reaches 85% of GDP, it is officially "bad" debt.

What does this mean for our fragile global economy? Let's turn to the data from the OECD's *Government at a Glance* to find out. According to that report, eleven OECD countries have debt that exceeds 85% of GDP:

- Japan, at 200%
- Greece, at 147%
- Italy, at 127%
- Iceland, at 126%
- Portugal, at 103%
- Ireland, at 102%
- Belgium, at 101%
- France, at 94%
- United States, also at 94%
- Germany, at 87%
- Hungary, at 86%

(As a matter of interest, Canada ranks twelfth in the standings, a smidge below the 85% danger level with total government debt equal to 84% of GDP. China is not a member of the OECD.)

That suggests any one — or more — of those eleven could be the pothole that takes the air out of our recovery.

But, of the many risks threatening the global economy, there are four that have the potential to create major disruptions: Europe, Japan, the United States and China.

---

6 Stephen G. Cecchetti, M.S. Mohanty and Fabrizio Zampolli, "The real effects of debt," *Bank for International Settlements Working Papers* No. 352 (September 2011).

Some Are More Indebted Than Others

Europe. Several of the Mediterranean countries that form part of the European Union (EU) have sizeable sovereign debt problems. Greece — with its "soft" debt restructuring, austerity program and rioting citizens — may grab the headlines but Greece is not the only problem in Europe. Ireland, Portugal, Spain, Belgium, the United Kingdom, France and Italy are all in trouble to some extent.

Although each of these countries has taken its own approach to dealing with its problems, still, these countries must operate within the bounds of the Eurozone and their common currency, the euro. That requires a common solution — and agreement from the member countries to adhere to that solution. As Craig Alexander, chief economist for TD Bank Group in Toronto, points out, execution is everything.[7] Can the seventeen members of the Eurozone "enact and implement" their rescue plans in a timely fashion?

Therein lies the risk. Should the member countries fail in their task, it could threaten the very survival of the EU. What happens when either a single nation or even a group of nations defaults? What impact would a failure of that magnitude have on the global economy? The effect is hard to predict, but were there to be a disorderly default by Greece, it could well become another Lehman Brothers moment, pushing the world's economy into a deep recession that governments would have little ability to counteract.

That is the worst-case scenario; the best-case scenario is that governments across the Eurozone will successfully curtail spending and reduce their annual deficits slowly. Slow growth, or no growth, will follow naturally from the reduction of government stimulus.

We will come back to Europe in the next chapter when we discuss in more detail the problems of using a single currency among a disparate group of nations, each with its own culture, history and economic realities.

United States. The second major financial risk to a tenuous recovery is that posed by the financial crisis in the U.S. The U.S.'s ability to derail any attempt at recovery was brought into sharp focus in the summer of 2011. As the U.S. government played political brinksmanship with the country's Triple A credit rating, the markets thrashed like a landed fish. The U.S. government's inability to forge a consensus on how to deal with its debt problems will be felt far into the future. The pessimists among us — or, perhaps, the

---

[7] Craig Alexander, "Paying the Piper," TD Bank Group, 28 September 2011, found at: www.td.com/economics, accessed 24 October 2011.

realists — conjecture that there will be no firm resolution to U.S. financial problems until after the November 2012 presidential election.

Although the public debate in the summer of 2011 was focused on the debt ceiling and the US$14.3 trillion of debt issued by the U.S. government (roughly 94% of the U.S.'s US$15-trillion economy as of June 30, 2011[8]), the public debt is only one aspect of a much larger issue: the U.S. has made more expensive commitments to its citizens in the form of future benefits than it can possibly provide. We will return to this important topic in Chapter 4.

Japan. The third major risk is on the other side of the world. Japan is rebuilding after the March 11, 2011, 9.0-magnitude earthquake and tsunami destroyed much of the infrastructure and industrial capacity of its northeast coastal region. A natural disaster of this magnitude would be tough for a country in solid financial shape. But even before the earthquake and tsunami struck, Japan was the world's most heavily indebted major economy, with a debt-to-GDP ratio of 200%. The cost of rebuilding the devastated portion of the country, coupled with the loss of tax revenue from the affected businesses and their employees, has only added to Japan's festering debt problem.

Yet, it was not so long ago that Japan was on the top of the world. The decade prior to 1989 saw Japan become an economic superpower, with its stock market and real estate markets surging to lofty heights. How, in one generation, did Japan go from the envy of the world to an economic basket case? What lessons can we learn from Japan's situation that can be applied to the problems facing the United States? What policy options does Japan have that will allow it to return to good economic health? And perhaps more importantly, what if Japan doesn't get a grip on its economic woes? The effects will rush through Western economies with the same deadly speed that the tsunami washed over northeastern Japan.

We will return to these issues in Chapter 5, as the problems facing Japan constitute one of the larger risks faced by the global financial community.

China. China has done an amazing job of modernizing its economy but that doesn't make it risk-free. It, too, may have an out-of-control real estate market headed for a crash and debt issues concealed by a lack of transparency. Any significant slowing of China's economy would put the brakes on a global recovery.

---

[8]   U.S. Department of Commerce, Bureau of Economic Analysis, found at: www.bea.gov, accessed 24 October 2011.

Starting with the reforms of Deng Xiaoping in the late 1970s, China has shifted gradually toward a capitalist economic system existing within a communist political system. The result has been the rapid modernization and industrialization of the Chinese economy which, in turn, has lifted hundreds of millions of Chinese citizens out of extreme poverty.

To get a sense of just how rapid this growth has been, let's look at annual per capita GDP. In 1990, China had annual per capita GDP of US$314, just 1.4% of U.S. annual per capita GDP of US$23,038. By 2010, annual per capita GDP in China had risen to US$4,393, or 9.3% of U.S. annual GDP in the same year of US$47,184. In the twenty-year period from 1990 to 2010, U.S. per capita GDP grew at an average annual rate of 3.65% while China's per capita GDP grew four times as fast, at an average annual rate of 14.1%.[9]

Following the onset of the global economic downturn in the fall of 2008, China opened the fiscal stimulus spigots and on November 9, 2008, introduced a four-trillion-yuan (US$586-billion) stimulus package. At about 14% of GDP, it was probably the largest peacetime stimulus ever.[10] The result was that China's economy rebounded quickly from the downturn. As the economies of the developed world stagnated under the deadening weight of debt, China has been the engine pulling the rest of the world with it. Its voracious appetite for commodities has benefitted the resources-exporting countries, especially Canada and Australia.

But what if that massive fiscal stimulus had an unintended effect? What if it created a real estate and investment bubble? And if there is a bubble, what if it bursts? Granted, those are a lot of "ifs" but it is a scenario that should be considered because the effects would reverberate throughout the global economy, especially in the countries that have benefitted from China's apparently insatiable appetite for raw materials (Canada and Australia). It could shatter our tentative global recovery and extend — once again — the length of the crisis.

We will investigate this possibility in Chapter 6.

---

[9] World Bank GDP per capita (current US$) data, found at: http://data.worldbank.org/indicator/NY.GDP.PCAP.CD/countries/CN-US-JP?display=default, accessed 24 October 2011.

[10] "Dr. Keynes's Chinese Patient," *The Economist* (13 November 2008), found at: www.economist.com/node/12601956, 24 October 2011.

What Can You Do to Recover?

- Understand that there are no quick fixes. Growth in most of the developed nations of the world will be anemic at best for the next few years, as governments face up to the overwhelming amounts of debt that is strangling their economies.
- Understand that the road to recovery is a bumpy one and a crisis in any one of the heavily indebted countries could destabilize and derail what is a very fragile recovery.
- Most importantly, get your own financial house in order. In the near term, recovery will begin at the individual household level, not at the macro or more global level.

CHAPTER 3

Europe:
Sovereigns on the Edge

THE PHRASE "SOVEREIGN DEBT CRISIS" says it all. Although we are all too familiar with Greece's solvency issues, Greece is not the only country in the Eurozone drowning in debt. Of the seventeen European Union (EU) members using the euro as a common currency,[1] Italy, Portugal, Spain, Ireland, Belgium, even France and Germany have too much sovereign debt when debt is taken as a percentage of gross domestic product (GDP).[2]

A report from Swiss bank UBS confirms how deep that sea of debt is. UBS Wealth Management Research showed sovereign debt-to-GDP ratios for 2011 ranging from a high of 166% (Greece) to a low of 6.6% (Estonia), with a Eurozone weighted average debt-to-GDP ratio of 88%.[3] The Maastricht Treaty, the legal contract that established the EU, stipulates a maximum debt-to-GDP ratio for any member country of 60%, a ceiling that has long since been razed.

In fact, debt in the Eurozone has expanded so quickly that the fear is no longer of a country defaulting; that's a matter of when, not if. The fear

---

[1] The seventeen EU countries using the euro are Belgium, Germany, Estonia, Ireland, Greece, Spain, France, Italy, Cyprus, Luxembourg, Malta, The Netherlands, Austria, Portugal, Slovenia, Slovakia and Finland.

[2] Organization for Economic Cooperation and Development, *Government at a Glance 2011*, p. 82.

[3] UBS Wealth Management Research, "Sovereign default in the Eurozone: Greece and Beyond," *Focus*, October 2011. Found at: http://www.ubs.com/1/e/wealthmanagement/wealth_management_research/ubs_research_focus.html, accessed 6 November 2011.

is "contagion," that the default of one country will spread uncontrollably to other deeply indebted countries in the EU, igniting a banking crisis and threatening the very survival of both the union and the currency. Although the disintegration of the EU appears unlikely, the mere fact that its demise has become the source of continuing speculation illustrates the very fragile nature of the global recovery.

Unfortunately, there is no easy, short-term solution to Europe's debt crisis. The easy choices were the ones not taken years ago; the only choices left now are the tough ones. To understand the present, however, we need to understand the past.

History Lesson

The integration of Europe began shortly after the Second World War when, in May 1949, ten countries that shared a determination to avoid the horrors of another world war — Belgium, Denmark, France, Ireland, Italy, Luxembourg, Netherlands, Norway, Sweden and the United Kingdom — created the Council of Europe. Its focus was to develop throughout Europe "common and democratic principles based on the European Convention on Human Rights and other reference texts on the protection of individuals."[4]

Shortly after the creation of the Council of Europe, some countries wanted to extend their shared focus to include trade. In 1951, Belgium, France, Germany, Italy, Luxembourg and The Netherlands created the European Coal and Steel Community. In 1957, the same group of nations formed the European Economic Community or "common market" and in 1973 Denmark, Ireland and the United Kingdom joined the original six. Greece joined in 1981 followed by Spain and Portugal in 1986. The intent was to foster trade and enhance growth by reducing economic barriers between countries.

In February 1992, the signing of the Maastricht Treaty in Maastricht, The Netherlands, established the European Union, built on the construct of a single market. The underlying concept of the EU was the freedom of movement of four categories: goods, services, people and money.

Austria, Finland and Sweden joined the EU in 1995, bringing the total to fifteen member nations. Cyprus, the Czech Republic, Estonia, Latvia, Lithuania, Hungary, Malta, Poland, Slovenia and Slovakia joined in 2004 and Bulgaria and Romania joined in 2007 — bringing the total to twenty-seven members. Along the way, the community expanded its political,

---

[4] Council of Europe, found at: http://www.coe.int/aboutCoe/index.asp?page=quisommesnous&l=en, accessed 6 November 2011. The Council now has forty-seven member countries and covers most of Europe.

economic and monetary scope. It introduced the common currency, the now-troubled euro, in 2002.

Four basic tenets contributed to the early success of the EU, according to Fraser Cameron, senior advisor, European Policy Centre, and adjunct professor, Hertie School of Governance in Berlin. In his paper entitled "The European Union as a Model for Regional Integration," published by the Council on Foreign Relations, Cameron identified these four tenets:[5]

- A "supranational community method" of politics, rather than the more traditional balance-of-power approach;
- The reconciliation between and leadership of France and Germany;
- The political will to share sovereignty and construct strong, legally based, common institutions to oversee integration;
- A consensus approach based on a willingness to help any member with a problem, the need for support of policies by the vast majority of members, and a willingness to provide financial help to poorer members.

It is, perhaps, the last of the four tenets that demands our attention in our troubled economic environment. As Greece flirted with default in 2011, EU members created the European Financial Stability Facility (EFSF). Its mandate: to safeguard financial stability in Europe by providing financial assistance to Eurozone member states by:

- providing loans to countries in financial difficulties;
- intervening in the secondary debt market when warranted;
- assisting in the recapitalization of financial institutions.

Over the course of 2011, the amount the EFSF was authorized to borrow went up in increments until it reached €1 trillion in October. How that plays out in 2012 will determine the survival of Greece and the extent of the impact on the EU and the Eurozone. But the continuing commitment to the tenet of shared financial assistance — amongst the others — speaks to the strength of the goals that brought the EU member nations together.

Day of Reckoning

Like most crises, the Eurozone's debt problem developed long before it reached crisis proportion. In fact, Cameron maintains, Europe's fiscal problems run deep and long. He points to twenty years of sluggish economic growth and the EU's declining share of global GDP, sliding to 22% in 2010 from 24% in 1990. Making matters worse, Europe's global competitiveness

---

[5] Fraser Cameron, "The European Union as a Model for Regional Integration," Council on Foreign Relations (September 2010), found at: http://www.cfr.org/eu/european-union-model-regional-integration/p22935#top, accessed 27 October 2011.

had weakened just as emerging markets such as Brazil, Russia, India and China were gaining traction.

At the root of the productivity problem were an aging work force with its attendant higher social costs, sclerotic and inflexible labour markets, insufficient resources devoted to innovation, and rising energy and commodity prices. Fixing the productivity problem was — and remains — neither easy nor fast.

It would be a mistake, however, to assume the EU and Eurozone members are a homogenous lot, all awash in debt and rendered uncompetitive. When the euro was introduced in 2002, and the member nations of the EU adopted a common currency, they did it from unequal footing. Some members — such as Germany and The Netherlands — were in good economic health and were internationally competitive. Germany's exports, for example, were strong and it had a growing balance of trade surplus. But the countries to the south — Greece, Portugal, Italy and, to a lesser degree, Spain — had low productivity and wages that were much too high for the output produced. In the years preceding the euro's introduction, they had not taken measures to become competitive, explains Patrick Leblond, associate professor of Public and International Affairs at the University of Ottawa in Ottawa. And, although the EU established standards for entry into the Eurozone, it appears they weren't followed.

Christopher Alessi, in his paper entitled "The Eurozone In Crisis," also published by the Council on Foreign Relations, notes that states wishing to enter the Eurozone had to meet several criteria including:

- ensuring inflation was no more than 1.5% a year;
- holding budget deficits at no more than 3% of GDP;
- maintaining a debt-to-GDP ratio of less than 60%.[6]

However, Alessi points out, the enforcement of these standards was inconsistent, even non-existent. He underscores his point by quoting hedge fund manager Jason Manolopoulos who, in his 2011 book *Greece's Odious Debt*, maintained: "There was shockingly weak due diligence in assessing the suitability for entry into the euro, and equally weak application of the few rules that were supposed to police its operation."[7]

Certainly, Italy, Spain and Greece were happy for the reprieve. Saddled with weaker economies and driven by domestic political considerations, leaders of these countries deferred the tough budgetary and restructuring

---

[6] Christopher Alessi, "The Eurozone In Crisis," Council on Foreign Relations (18 October 2011) found at: http://www.cfr.org/eu/eurozone-crisis/p22055, accessed 27 October 2011.

[7] Jason Manolopoulos, *Greece's Odious Debt: The Looting of the Hellenic Republic by the Euro, the Political Elite and the Investment Community* (London: Anthem Press, 2011).

measures that were needed to meet the requirements. All three entered the Eurozone without the economic fundamentals that would have allowed them to withstand the shock of unsettled times. And thanks to the infusion of cash and cheap credit from other Eurozone members, once inside they were able to put off the day of reckoning even further.

Leblond argues that even then, once inside the Eurozone, it would have made sense for those countries to institute the economic and structural reforms that would have made their economies more productive and competitive. But they didn't! At the same time, these nations became less and less competitive as their wages and the cost of doing business became more and more expensive.

As members of the Eurozone, however, their ability to manoeuvre was limited. Before adopting the euro, these southern countries had solved some of their economic problems by devaluating their currencies or allowing inflation. It is much easier to enhance productivity by allowing inflation to rise more quickly than wages than it is to cut wages. Once inside the Eurozone, however, currency devaluation and inflation were no longer options; the member nations no longer controlled their own monetary policies. The only adjustment mechanism available to the less productive countries was to cut wages drastically to reflect the lower output per labour hour compared with the more productive countries of the north.

In 2011, Greece became the first of the southern nations to suffer the effects of past policies publicly. As the EU demanded austerity as a condition for bailouts, government expenditures were dramatically curtailed. As government expenditures fell and as government workers were laid off, aggregate demand within the economy diminished. As aggregate demand fell, businesses sold less and workers worked fewer hours. National income and tax receipts crumbled, compounding the initial problem of high government deficits. As anyone with a television or the internet knows, Greece crumbled into disarray.

As Greece discovered, when budget deficits are slashed too quickly, the result is often a worsening of the budget deficit in the future.

In a robust economy, the ideal situation would see economic growth outpace the increase in debt, allowing a country's debt-to-GDP ratio to decline, even if the absolute amount of debt continues to rise. The 60% cap on the debt-to-GDP ratio imposed by the Maastricht Treaty was intended to ensure that, under normal conditions of economic growth and interest rates, debt would never grow faster than GDP.

But Europe's economic circumstances are less than ideal. The ability of Greece and, to some extent, Italy, Portugal, Spain and Ireland to grow their GDPs faster than their debt is increasingly constrained if not downright impossible. The higher interest rates imposed on those with higher levels of debt makes it ever more difficult to outrun the debt monster. This is the situation in the weaker Eurozone countries today. With the inflation option off the table, Greece is left with only one plausible solution to its debt problem — it has to reduce the actual amount of debt to a level that the economy can support.

As of early November 2011, Greece had central government debt of €338 billion (US$442 billion) and GDP of US$300 billion. To reach the 60% debt-to-GDP limit imposed under the Maastricht Treaty, Greece would have to reduce its debt by some US$260 billion. Unfortunately there is no easy way to accomplish this task, as for every dollar of debt written off by Greece, a corresponding lender has to write off a dollar of financial assets.

The danger lies in a disorderly default by Greece. Were that to happen, interest rates on debt issued by the weaker members of the EU would certainly spike higher, as lenders anticipated that they, too, might choose a debt default as the best way out. And as borrowing costs rise, budget deficits widen and debt-to-GDP ratios ratchet higher.

To go back to the UBS Wealth Management Research report, it calls Greece "unambiguously insolvent" and expects a default in the spring of 2012. But it is betting on a more-or-less orderly default:

> If Eurozone parliaments approve the reform of the rescue mechanism in time, this should help to ring-fence other vulnerable countries and systemically important banks. The question on everyone's mind nevertheless remains: can these measures contain the contagion to other countries, or will a full default in Greece cause the debt crisis to escalate out of control? Our base case assumes that the contagion will be contained eventually — although this containment could come at substantial monetary and political cost.[8]

The Road Ahead

There are no easy remedies for the problems besetting the Eurozone. The entire area drank heavily from the debt trough for many years, with debt levels rising faster than GDP. As any partygoer knows, you can only delay the hangover for so long; the longer you defer it, the worse you will

---

[8] UBS Wealth Management Research, "Sovereign default in the Eurozone: Greece and Beyond."

eventually feel. Europe is finally suffering the hangover. To quote TD Bank Group chief economist Craig Alexander:

> The main message is that the European fiscal crisis will not be solved in the short-term. Even fiscal integration and jointly issued European bonds could not remedy the fundamental problem at the root of the Eurozone crisis: too much public and private debt and extremely poor economic growth potential.[9]

Many questions remain, irrespective of how the member states resolve the sovereign debt crisis that dominated European financial news throughout 2011. For starters, will they put mechanisms in place to prevent a replay? Is there the political will to return the EU to its former lofty goals? Or have governments become so distracted with fighting fires that prevention of future fires is being delayed for another day? Alternately, will Greece decide to exit the EU and face its fate with its own currency and monetary policy?

Perhaps there is a silver lining in Europe's dark cloud. The sovereign debt crisis may give the EU's financially disciplined members the means to force its debt-ridden members to undertake long-delayed fiscal and structural reforms. In that event, the troubled nations could emerge stronger and more competitive and, in time, contribute to the economic strength of the EU.

What Can You Do to Recover?

- Expect continued volatility in Europe as the troubled EU countries lurch from crisis to crisis. The instability in Europe will continue to add to the fragility of our global economy.
- Investment opportunities in Europe will be few and far between as the "PIIGS" — Portugal, Italy, Ireland, Greece and Spain — are pushed to restructure and refinance. Even among the stronger nations, there will be drags on growth as they put financial and intellectual effort into rescuing their fellow Eurozone members. So, avoid or minimize Europe's weighting in your portfolio.
- On a personal level, there is not much you can do about Europe's sovereign debt crisis, other than protect yourself from the inevitable fallout. You can, however, learn from their mistakes and ensure that it does not happen to you. If your household is fuelled by debt, you too could go up in flames. You can't hear this enough: get your own fiscal house in order.

---

[9] Craig Alexander, "Paying the Piper," TD Bank Group (28 September 2011).

CHAPTER 4

United States:
The Ailing Giant

IT IS HARD TO IDENTIFY one single culprit in the cataclysmic events of 2008, but certainly easy, cheap credit is a strong contender. It was easy credit in the U.S. that motivated short-sighted, profit-driven bankers to give mortgages to people who could not afford them; it was easy pickings that drove profit-driven investment banks to securitize these "assets" and sell them globally. So, when those mortgage holders began to default, the repercussions were felt around the world. Only then did the world take stock of the role debt had played in the crisis.

Our neighbour to the south — the biggest economy in the world — is wallowing in debt. By August 2011, when the poisonous debates about the U.S. debt ceiling derailed a fragile recovery, the U.S. government had accumulated US$14.3 trillion in federal debt, or 94% of its US$15-trillion economy. For the year ended September 30, 2011, the U.S. reported a budget deficit of US$1.3 trillion, or 8.6% of GDP.

But that is history. Ahead is the need for U.S. politicians to form a credible plan to contain that debt, which will be a challenge given the U.S. debt burden is growing at a faster pace than its GDP. And, unfortunately, the debt already issued is only a small portion of the future commitments the U.S. has made to its citizens — promises that almost certainly cannot be kept.

Quantitative Easing and Other Measures

The failure of Lehman Brothers on September 15, 2008, sent shock waves throughout the world. In the following months, even as the U.S. economy plunged into recession, the U.S. central bank, the Federal Reserve, took heroic measures to save the global economy from total collapse.

The Fed had already begun a policy of monetary easing, that is, increasing the supply of money in the economy, by dropping the rate at which the Fed lends money to banks. Over the course of the previous year, the target range for the federal funds rate[1] dropped by increments to 1% by October 29, 2008, from 5.25% in September 2007. With the economy showing increasing stress, however, the Fed dropped the funds rate again on December 16, 2008, this time by 1%, bringing the target range to 0%–0.25%, the lowest in its history. (And that is where the range has remained and will remain. The Federal Open Market Committee, as it stated in a November 2, 2011, press release, "currently anticipates that economic conditions — including low rates of resource utilization and a subdued outlook for inflation over the medium run — are likely to warrant exceptionally low levels for the federal funds rate at least through mid-2013."[2])

But the Fed went far beyond traditional monetary policy in 2008 as it attempted to resuscitate an ailing economy. It dramatically expanded both its balance sheet and its arsenal of policy tools, introducing a variety of innovative — and expensive — solutions. For example, the Agency Mortgage-backed Securities Purchase Program entailed purchasing the debt of government-sponsored entities, the Federal National Mortgage Association or "Fannie Mae" and the Federal Home Mortgage Corporation or "Freddie Mac." The two were the largest mortgage finance lenders in the U.S. and at the heart of the subprime mortgage fiasco. In time, the U.S. put Fannie Mae and Freddie Mac into conservatorship, a form of receivership.

Also among its arsenal were programs meant to boost liquidity. With the Term Auction Facility, the Fed auctioned collaterized term loans to deposit-taking institutions in good standing at lower than discount rates, creating a so-called "discount window" and boosting bankers' liquidity. The Term Securities Lending Facility loaned U.S. Treasury securities for one-month terms to "primary dealers" while the Primary Dealer Credit Facility provided overnight cash against eligible collateral.

---

[1]   The target for the federal funds rate is the rate at which the Federal Reserve would like to see banks lend to each other on an overnight basis.

[2]   Board of Governors of the Federal Reserve System, 2011 Monetary Policy Releases, 2 November 2011, found at: http://www.federalreserve.gov/newsevents/press/monetary/20111102a.htm, accessed 10 November 2011.

That is just a sampling of the programs that put more money into the system. As well, to promote stability, the Fed forced the largest banks in the country to accept additions to their capital, even if they didn't want it.

These actions kept our fragile world from shattering, all the while driving the U.S. deeper into debt.

One of the more controversial tools used by the Fed was "quantitative easing" (QE), which increases the supply of money in an economy by, essentially, printing money.

Here's how it works. The central bank "monetizes" the debt of the government, that is, the bank exchanges a liability that is not money for a liability that is money. Say the U.S. government issues a new security — a Treasury bill, a Treasury note or a Treasury bond. That becomes a liability of the government that is not money. The Fed purchases the new security, thereby creating a liability on its balance sheet that is equal to the value of the government security purchased. New "money" has come into existence; the money supply has increased by the amount of the purchase of government debt, even though this new money is really just a liability of the central bank.

But this new money has a compounding effect. As it enters the economy through the banking system, it is loaned out, then deposited, becoming the basis for another loan, which gets deposited, and so on. Soon, this new money is held in the form of reserves somewhere in the banking system. When the process works as intended, the eventual increase in money supply is equal to the amount of new money created divided by the reserve ratio of the banking system. So, if banks keep 10% of all deposits in the form of reserves, a $1-million injection of new money into the economy by the central bank will eventually result in a $10-million increase in the money supply.

Why would the central bank want to create new money? To stimulate economic activity by pushing down interest rates which, in turn, induces people to borrow and spend, which increases economic activity. The process is successful to the extent that the funds end up in the economic system where they generate jobs and foster consumer and capital purchases. When QE works as intended, therefore, it stimulates growth and boosts investor confidence.

During 2008-2009, the Fed undertook its first round of quantitative easing (QE1), injecting US$600 billion into the economy — that later increased to US$2.1 trillion — by buying up debt securities issued by both the government and financial institutions. In November 2010, it launched

QE2, injecting another US$600 billion into the economy. Together QE1 and QE2 tripled the size of the Fed's balance sheet.

Unfortunately, maintains James Awad, a forty-two-year veteran of capital management and managing director of New York-based Zephyr Management LP, the process had limited success. He concedes QE1 saved the American financial system from imploding in the early years of the crisis, and he acknowledges that the easing process unlocked the strangle-hold on liquidity and saved specific companies and industries from sure disaster, but at what price?

"We will never how efficiently the money was spent or what would have happened if the Fed hadn't done it," Awad says. "We were in a downward spiral worldwide and, for better or for worse, it appears in retrospect that it did arrest that spiral."

The long-term effect of QE2 is more questionable. Once more, cheap and plentiful credit goaded investors into buying riskier assets than they otherwise might have, boosting the feeling of wealth in the financial sector — the banks, insurance companies and hedge funds that provided those products. QE2, however, did little to help wages or employment in the non-financial sector. "In fact, in many ways you could say it hurt the non-capital sector because unemployment remained high," says Awad. "Wages were stagnant and, in real terms, had been going down. In some cases, the poor were paying more for food, energy and commodities because much of the extra liquidity was leaking into speculation in commodities and asset prices. In many ways, QE2 helped the financial sector and hurt the non-financial sector."

In retrospect, the two rounds of quantitative easing did not provide a sufficient catalyst to reinvigorate the economy, although there were some short-term effects. But long-term, there was little in the way of permanent job creation and income generation. Instead of new tax revenues, all the U.S. got was more debt — and an unsettling sense that it was headed down the same path Japan took twenty years previously.

The next major intervention by the Fed, "Operation Twist," began in October 2011. It was designed to push down yields at the long end of the interest rate curve. By increasing demand for long-dated government bonds, long bond prices would move higher; as prices went up, long bonds yields would fall.

The intent was to make long-term borrowing cheaper, thus encour-aging companies to borrow and invest in new, employment-enhancing plants and equipment. Although lower long-term interest rates are benefi-cial for consumers and the goods-producing sector, the effect on financial institutions' profitability is exactly the opposite. When long interest rates are low, banks face a narrower spread between the cost of their short-term borrowing and their long-term lending activities, making it harder to generate profits. In a fragile economic climate, lower profits can be problematic.

The impact of Operation Twist has been mixed. Long bond yields did move down significantly in anticipation of Operation Twist, to 2.75% on October 3 from 3.8% in early August. But by the end of October 2011, thirty-year U.S. government bond yields had regained lost ground and were yielding 3.45%.

Despite the heroic efforts of the Fed, the U.S. economy starts 2012 deep in a debt-induced funk. Unemployment remains elevated at more than 9%, and close to 20% of the potential working population is either unemployed, underemployed or working part-time. Residential real estate prices have shown little to no strength, leaving about 25% of U.S. families holding mortgages worth more than the value of their homes.[3] Real GDP per capita is back at 2005 levels, real wages are flat or falling and consumer confidence is low. And there is no end in sight.

Debt: How Bad Is It?

The U.S. has a treacherous road ahead. One deadline passes, only to be followed by another, as the U.S. lurches from crisis to crisis like a vehicle running out of gas. The competing factions in the government may reach a short-term resolution but the problem isn't solved. It is like raising an individual's credit card limit. The day of reckoning may be averted but the debt remains unpaid — and interest charges keep accruing.

So, how bad is it? As 2011 drew to a close, U.S. national debt — that is, the face value or principal amount of marketable and non-marketable securities outstanding — was US$15 trillion, the equivalent of US$132,700 per taxpayer.[4] Add in household debt, business debt, financial institutions' debt and debt from federal, state and local governments and the total reached US$54.5 trillion. (Personal debt alone was US$16 trillion — more than the U.S. national debt!)

But that is only one part of the U.S. government's problem. Unfunded liabilities for entitlement programs — those programs that provide the social safety net for the U.S.'s 312 million-plus people, 78 million of whom

---

3   David Rhodes and Daniel Stelter, *Stop Kicking the Can Down the Road: The price of not address-ing the root causes of the crisis*, Boston Consulting Group (August 2011), found at: http://www.bcg.com/expertise_impact/publications/PublicationDetails.aspx?id=tcm:12-83769, accessed 11 November 2011.

4   The U.S. National Debt Clock found at: http://www.usdebtclock.org, accessed 31 October 2011.

are baby boomers — were US$116 trillion in 2011. Social security accounted for US$15.3 trillion of that, prescription drug programs US$20.3 trillion and Medicare US$80.6 trillion. And if we take the present value difference between projected revenue and projected spending to meet future promises made to those citizens by the U.S. government, we have a "fiscal gap" of US$202 trillion,[5] or about 13.5 times U.S. GDP. Put another way, the U.S. government has made promises that exceed its ability to pay by about US$650,000 per man, woman and child living in the United States.

In order to close this fiscal gap, the International Monetary Fund estimated in its July 2010 *Selected Issues Paper*, the U.S. would require a fiscal adjustment equal to 14% of GDP or a doubling of all U.S. taxes. That would produce a budget surplus equal to 5.5% of GDP,[6] which the U.S. needs for several years to come if it is meet its spending commitments. Does that sound like a likely prospect in a country addicted to debt?

Put this up against a political debate about debt that has been, at best, divisive and, at worst, venomous, and you have substantial roadblocks to global economic recovery.

The Forecast is Cloudy

What are the implications of all this debt? Let's first look at American consumers and the US$16 trillion in personal debt they have accumulated in mortgages, car loans and credit card debt. U.S. consumers were living on borrowed time; these heavily indebted individuals need to pay down debts — or "deleverage" — and increase savings. When a consumer substitutes debt repayment for spending, economic activity declines, unless another economic sector makes up the difference. So far, the other sector has been the U.S. government, but its ability to keep spending has become severely constrained.

"That automatically causes a massive contraction in the country's GDP," says Tom O'Gorman, director of fixed income at Calgary-based Bissett Investment Management, part of Franklin Templeton Investments Corp.

The U.S. consumers' ability to repay debt has been and will continue to be hampered by unemployment. It is hard to pay down debt when you don't have income. And in an environment of economic instability, even those who are employed may fear for their jobs. Caution will dictate they curtail discretionary purchases such as travel and entertainment.

---

[5] Laurence Kotlikoff, "U.S. is bankrupt and we don't even know it," Bloombery LP (10 August 2010), found at: http://www.bloomberg.com/news/2010-08-11/u-s-is-bankrupt-and-we-don-t-even-know-commentary-by-laurence-kotlikoff.html, accessed 11 November 2011.

[6] Ibid.

Just getting a handle on the level of unemployment is difficult. Taking into account individuals not included in the official figures, O'Gorman puts unemployment between 15% and 20%. "If people have dropped out of the work force they're not counted," he says. "Where did all those people go? They didn't all retire."

The problem extends beyond the obvious. For example, the disastrous housing market has meant a huge chunk of jobs has disappeared from the construction sector. But it has also affected professionals such as the analysts and lawyers who, before the meltdown, worked on securitizing and packaging the mortgages. Those jobs have disappeared.

"Those jobs are gone and they're never coming back," O'Gorman says.

U.S. government debt and the U.S.'s ability to control it provide a similarly gloomy picture. According to the Bank for International Settlements, when the ratio of government debt to GDP exceeds 85%, it puts a drag on future economic growth. The U.S.'s government debt-to-GDP ratio was about 100% at yearend 2011 and getting worse. Should the U.S. fail to get its debt under control, eventually the bond market will force the issue, much as it did in Greece and Italy. When that day might come is never known, until it occurs, which makes it even more important for the U.S. to take action sooner rather than later.

The implications of too much U.S. debt are many. "As long as there is loose monetary policy in the U.S. and no credible fiscal plan in place," says Camilla Sutton, senior currency strategist at Toronto-based Scotia Capital Inc., "it spells a story of U.S.-dollar weakness."

For at least a decade, analysts have speculated that the American dollar could lose its status as the world's reserve currency. Sutton believes that transition could take another decade. The shift has not yet occurred because the U.S. has the world's deepest bond market, she says. That means that reserve flows looking for liquidity gravitate toward it. China, often cited as a candidate for the next holder of the world's reserve currency, does not have a well-developed bond market — yet.

The U.S. economy has huge challenges ahead — massive debt that inhibits spending, unfunded liabilities that can only add to social discontent and unrest, and a fractious government that makes any resolution difficult. And 2012 is an election year, which will further impede progress. It is likely the U.S. will be a drag on global growth for some time to come.

What Can You Do to Recover?

- U.S. government and personal debt will be a drag on global growth. Your personal recovery means understanding the stresses and strains in the U.S. economy, then looking at their impact on your financial situation.
- The U.S. is likely to remain Canada's most important trading partner but commodities demand from emerging markets such as China has become more important than in the past. "The U.S. will be marginally less important as Canada's trading partner than it has been," says Awad, "and the emerging markets will be more important."
- In the modern global economy you cannot eliminate the impact of foreign events by avoiding equity exposure to a specific region. But you can insulate your portfolio to a certain extent by being properly diversified from an asset and geographical perspective.

CHAPTER 5

Japan: A Lesson in What Not to Do

THE PLIGHT OF JAPAN strikes fear into the hearts of politicians trying to extricate their countries from the worst global economic downturn since the 1930s. Perhaps more so as Japan, not so very long ago, was the envy of the developed world. But that was before it suffered two decades of economic dislocation. Now, Japan has the highest debt-to-GDP ratio in the developed world.

But Japan is more than the story of one country's slide into economic stagnation. It is also a cautionary tale to which investors and policy makers need to pay heed, because the conditions that led to Japan's "lost decade" have many parallels in today's economic climate.

The Post-War Growth Period

The Second World War destroyed much of Japan's industrial capacity and, by 1945, the defeated Japan was an economic invalid, its economy wracked by widespread shortages, rampant inflation and a devalued currency. From 1945 to 1952, the U.S. occupied Japan; with the backing of significant U.S. aid and the efforts of a highly disciplined and well-educated work force, Japan quickly began building a modern industrial economy.

The process of rebuilding was facilitated by protective tariffs and a government-induced culture of household savings. These savings, channeled through the traditional banking sector, provided plenty of loanable funds to Japanese firms wanting to borrow to invest in growth. And invest they did. Throughout the entire post-war period, Japan invested heavily in new production capacity. Investment in new capital assets averaged 20% of gross national product (GNP)[1] in the 1950s and grew to more than 30% of GNP in the 1960s and 1970s. In the latter part of the 1980s, in the lead-up to the bubble years, capital investment retrenched to around 20%.[2]

Because of the almost-complete destruction of Japanese industry during the war, Japanese businesses literally started over. With strong government backing and direction, they imported the latest technologies. They also learned from and avoided some of the common mistakes made by nations further along the industrialization curve. This heavy investment in new, highly efficient industrial capacity, followed by large investments in research and development, allowed Japan — a country with few natural resources — to move from being a producer of cheap, low-quality goods to a world leader in high-quality, technologically advanced manufactured goods.

By the mid-1980s, Japanese industry had become the envy of the industrialized world. In the space of thirty years, "Made in Japan" had gone from a derogatory term denoting low quality to a sign of respect signifying innovation and craftsmanship. Japan assumed leadership in consumer electronics, the automobile industry, manufacturing and robotics, arousing in the Western World a slight unease with Japanese dominance.[3]

But what an amazing story of growth and development it was. Throughout the 1970s, Japan's gross domestic product (GDP) was second only to the United States'. By 1990, its per capita GDP had grown to US$24,754 from US$9,068 in 1980, making Japan first among major industrialized nations. By comparison, in 1990, Canada had per capita GDP of US$20,968 and the U.S., US$23,038.[4]

A belief developed that Japan had somehow unlocked the secret to perpetual economic prosperity through a "third way," a form of economics that fell somewhere between free market capitalism and a centrally planned economy. Government and corporations appeared to act cooperatively to achieve mutual benefit. Bureaucracies planned and coordinated

---

[1] Gross domestic product (GDP) and GNP are closely related. GDP is the total value of what a country produces over the course of one year. GNP is equal to GDP plus the amount earned from assets held in other countries minus the amount earned by foreigners who own assets domestically.

[2] "Economic History of Japan," found at: http://en.wikipedia.org/wiki/Economic_history_of_Japan, accessed 31 October 2011.

[3] Mark Thornton, "The Japanese Bubble Economy," 23 May 2004, found at: www.lewrockwell.com/thornton/thornton24.html, accessed 28 October 2011.

[4] "GDP per Capita," The World Bank, found at: http://data.worldbank.org/indicator/NY.GDP.PCAP.CD?page=4, accessed 28 October 2011.

the economy through the use of liberally applied incentives and tax breaks, directing investment in profitable directions. Japanese management was said to spur innovation, enhance product quality and reliability, and capture large market for its exports.[5]

At the same time, soaring land and stock market values allowed Japanese firms and individuals to invest heavily in other countries, sometime invoking fear of Japanese economic imperialism.

The bubble period in Japan began in September 1985 with the signing of the Plaza Accord. Named after the Plaza Hotel in New York City where the agreement was signed, the Plaza Accord was an attempt by the governments of France, West Germany, Japan, the United States and the United Kingdom to depreciate the U.S. dollar in relation to the Japanese yen and the German Deutsche Mark. Faced with roaring inflation throughout the latter part of the 1970s, the U.S. central bank, under the leadership of Paul Volcker, had raised interest rates, sending the U.S. dollar flying but putting the U.S. economy into a deep, double-dip recession. From 1980 to 1985, the currency had appreciated by approximately 50% against the yen, Deutsche Mark and the British pound.[6] The result was a profoundly uncompetitive U.S. economy, with goods manufactured in other countries priced much lower, in U.S. dollars, than U.S. manufactured goods.

The Plaza Accord, along with the Baker-Miyazawa Agreement in 1986 and the Louvre Accord in 1987, committed the Bank of Japan to policies designed to stimulate the Japanese domestic economy as a means of supporting the U.S. economic recovery. The Bank of Japan lowered interest rates, making it cheaper for individuals and businesses to borrow. From January 1986 to February 1987, the central bank reduced its official discount rate five times, bringing it to 2.5%, where it would remain until May 1989.[7] This reduction in Japanese interest rates had exactly the desired effect of stimulating domestic demand, but it also caused the yen to depreciate against other currencies, making Japanese exports more competitive and imports more expensive.

The Japanese stock market responded to the dropping yen with a massive rally, accelerating a trend that had begun in 1984. By early 1987, the Nikkei 225 index, a proxy for the Japanese market, was around 20,000. The stock market collapse of October 1987 slowed the rise but only temporarily. By the close of the following year, the Nikkei surpassed 30,000, a 39%

---

[5] Thornton, "The Japanese Bubble Economy."
[6] "The Plaza Accord," found at http://en.wikipedia.org/wiki/Plaza_Accord, accessed October 28, 2011.
[7] Geoffrey P. Miller, "The Role of a Central Bank in a Bubble Economy," *Cardozo Law Review*, Vol. 18, No 3, (December 1996).

increase for the year. By the beginning of 1989, the market value of stocks traded on Japanese stock markets accounted for more than 42% of the market value of all stocks globally, up from 15% in 1980.[8]

In bubbles, investors generally find a way to convince themselves that this time is different, that overheated valuations are fundamentally sound. Japan in the late 1980s was no different. The economy was racing ahead, unemployment was negligible at 2.2% and inflation was insignificant. Japan appeared to have found economic nirvana, with full employment, low inflation, high economic growth, a large trade surplus and huge increases in share prices and property markets. Warning signs, such as share prices far higher than corporate earnings warranted (the price/earnings or P/E ratio) went unheeded. At the end of 1988, the average P/E ratio was an astronomical 58.67, compared to a long-term average P/E for the Standard & Poor's 500 composite index of fifteen. To put this number into perspective, it would take a Japanese investor almost fifty-nine years to recover the price paid for a stock from company earnings.

Japanese real estate followed a similar trajectory, with prices more than doubling in a four-year period. In 1988 alone, residential property prices rose by 70% year over year, while commercial real estate prices climbed 80%. Choice properties in Tokyo's Ginza district were selling for as much as US$1.5 million per square meter (US$139,000 per square foot).[9]

By 1989, the bubble in Japanese land and stock market valuations was full blown and investors were leveraging their gains. Investors posted rapidly rising shares as collateral for property loans; the property thus acquired was used as collateral for loans to purchase more shares. Loans were easily accessible as younger Japanese, unable to afford real estate, banked their savings; the banks recycled those deposits into additional loans. Because of rising share prices, the banks were able to issue new common stock at very high prices, allowing them to lend even more.

The Bursting of the Bubble

The Bank of Japan began to tighten monetary policy in May 1989, increasing interest rates to cool an overheating economy. That month, the official discount rate moved to 3.25% from 2.5%, the first hike in nine years. In October, it raised the official discount rate again, to 3.75%.[10] The Japanese central bank had finally moved to cool off the Japanese economy, although it was too little too late.

---

[8] Ibid.
[9] "Economic History of Japan," Wikipedia.
[10] Miller, "The Role of a Central Bank in a Bubble Economy."

August 1990 brought the Iraqi invasion of Kuwait, destabilizing equity markets, and investors began to worry about war, inflation and higher oil prices. The air was coming out of the Japanese bubble; the Nikkei lost 11% in a single day, then stabilized briefly.

Although we talk about the bubble "bursting," that wasn't exactly the case. Both real estate and stock prices deflated over a long period of time. The Nikkei fell sharply for two and one-half years, losing 63% of its value and reaching 14,309 in August 1992, before bottoming in April 2003 at 7,607 — an 80% drop from its 1990 peak. It has never recovered.

Japanese real estate suffered a similarly spectacular fall. Japanese commercial real estate values began falling in 1991 and eroded steadily for the next 16 years.[11] Those values never recovered. By 2007, average commercial real estate prices were well below their 1974 levels.

That collapse ushered in a severe economic downturn which resulted in what economist and author Geoffrey Miller calls "the most serious instability in the financial system since the 1920s."[12] Companies that had over-invested in plants, equipment and inventory during the bubble years were left with a large overhang of unsold goods, which made new output unnecessary. Consumers, seeing their net worth vanish, spent less and saved more. Demand dropped.

The bursting of the stock market and real estate bubbles in the first half of the 1990s was aggravated by a rapidly appreciating yen. The yen rose to 80-85 yen to one U.S. dollar in the spring of 1995 from 150 yen to one U.S. dollar in 1990. For a country dependent on exports, this went a long way to pricing Japanese products right out of the global market.

Japan's central bank responded to the downturn in the summer of 1991 by dropping the official discount rate to 5.5% from 6.0%. It then continued to cut the official discount rate until it reached a historic low of 1% in April 1995. But the economy didn't respond to the monetary stimulus of low interest rates. The rate of growth in nominal GDP, which had been as high as 7% a year during the bubble years, flat-lined from 1991 to 1993.

When the credit-induced stock and real estate bubble burst, Japan entered what today we would call a "balance sheet" or "deleveraging" recession. Individuals and corporations had watched the value of their assets collapse while the liability side of the balance sheet — their debts — had remained at pre-collapse levels. If they were to avoid insolvency, they had to repair their balance sheets by paying down debt. As each sector of the economy reduced spending and borrowing, consumption

---

[11] Japan Ministry of Land, Infrastructure, Transport and Tourism.
[12] Miller, "The Role of a Central Bank in a Bubble Economy."

and investment fell and the economy slowed even more. In response, the government of Japan began a series of stimulus programs meant to revive the economy by replacing private sector demand with public spending. Between 1990 and 2008, the Japanese government introduced fifteen fiscal stimulus packages, the key components of which included:

- public works and social infrastructure projects, including land acquisition (14.2% of 2000 GDP);
- credit guarantees and augmentation of credit lines to banks for loans to small and medium-sized enterprises and for the housing sector (8.5% of GDP);
- employment assistance and cash transfers (2.1% of GDP); and
- tax measures (3.3% of GDP).[13]

The stimulus spending didn't work; economic activity didn't pick up, or when it did, the effect was only temporarily. Government spending was never offset by increased revenue in the form of tax receipts. The result was a constantly growing federal debt, shown as a percentage of GDP in the following table.

Government Debt as a Percentage of Gross Domestic Product

	1990	1995	2000	2005	2009
Japan	47.0%	65.2%	106.1%	164.5%	183.5%
Canada	46.6%	56.8%	40.1%	30.2%	35.7%

Source: Organization for Economic Cooperation and Development.[14]

And it has only gotten worse. Japan spent large amounts of cash to stimulate the economy and counteract the downturn of 2008-2009. By OECD reckoning, in 2010, Japan's gross-debt-to-GDP ratio hit 200%;[15] *The Economist* suggests that ratio may have reached 228% by the end of 2011.[16]

Is this the fate that awaits Western nations that have likewise accumulated large and growing debt, ratcheting up debt-to-GDP ratios?

---

[13] Markus Brückner and Anita Tuladhar, "Public Investment as a Fiscal Stimulus: Evidence from Japan's Regional Spending During the 1990s," International Monetary Fund *Working Paper* (April, 2010).

[14] Organization for Economic Cooperation and Development "StatExtracts" online database, total central government debt, found at http://stats.oecd.org/index.aspx?DataSetCode=GOV_DEBT, accessed 1 November 2011.

[15] Organization for Economic Cooperation and Development, *Government at a Glance 2011* (Paris, 2011), p. 83.

[16] "How will Japan pay for reconstruction," *The Economist*, 14 March 2011, found at: http://www.economist.com/blogs/freeexchange/2011/03/sovereign_debt, accessed 2 November 2011.

The problem in Japan, maintains Richard Koo, the respected chief economist of Japan's Nomura Research Institute, was not the stimulus spending per se, but the fact that it was constantly being withdrawn before the economy had stabilized. As he wrote in *The Economist*:

When the deficit hawks manage to remove the fiscal stimulus while the private sector is still deleveraging, the economy collapses and re-enters the deflationary spiral. That weakness, in turn, prompts another fiscal stimulus, only to see it removed again by the deficit hawks once the economy stabilizes. This unfortunate cycle can go on for years if the experience of post-1990 Japan is any guide. The net result is that the economy remains in the doldrums for years, and many unemployed workers will never find jobs in what appears to be structural unemployment, even though there is nothing structural about their predicament. Japan took fifteen years to come out of its balance sheet recession because of this unfortunate cycle where the necessary medicine was applied only intermittently.

The real impediment to a sustained recovery from a balance sheet recession, therefore, is the inability of orthodox academics and policy makers to accept the fact that the private sector is minimizing debt and that their aversion to fiscal stimulus based on the assumption that the private sector is maximizing profits is unwarranted. If Japan had known that it had actually contracted a different disease and kept its fiscal stimulus in place until the private sector balance sheets were repaired, it would have recovered from the recession much faster and at a much lower cost than the 460 trillion yen or US$5 trillion it eventually took to cure the disease.[17]

If Koo is correct, Japan's long period of deflation and stagnation was the result of bad implementation, not bad policy. But the end result is still a ballooning debt that has to be funded. And therein lies the threat that Japan presents to our fragile global recovery.

Japan's Savings Crisis

Japan is speeding toward a savings crisis that could create a massive pile-up on the road to recovery. As Martin Feldstein, professor of economics at Harvard University and former chairman of President Ronald Reagan's

---

[17] Richard Koo, "America lacks the necessary commitment to stimulus," *The Economist*, 26 July 2010, found at: http://www.economist.com/economics/by-invitation/guest-contributions/no_america_lacks_necessary_commitment_stimulus, accessed 2 November 2011.

Council of Economic Advisors, sees it: "The potential future clash between larger fiscal deficits and a low household saving rate could have powerful negative effects on both Japan and the global economy."[18]

In a 2010 article, Feldstein tracks the declining household savings rate in Japan, from 15% of after-tax income in the flush 1980s, to 10% in the post-collapse 1990s, ending that decade at 5%, before settling at slightly more than 2% in 2009.

Low household savings coupled with massive government debt would normally force a country to borrow from the rest of the world, says Feldstein. But not Japan; thanks to a high corporate savings rate and low residential and non-residential fixed investment, Japan maintains a current-account surplus, putting Japan in a position to provide billions of dollars for other countries to borrow. In 2010 Japan sent more than 3% of its GDP abroad. "Japan's national savings still exceed its domestic investment, allowing Japan to be a net capital exporter," concludes Feldstein.

That excess of national savings over investment has another questionable effect. It keeps Japan's long-term interest rates so low they are almost negligible.

So what are the risks with this scenario? Either rising interest rates, brought on by the advent of inflation, or declining net business savings could end Japan's current-account surplus. With debt in excess of 200% of its GDP, a two-percentage-point hike in interest rates would boost Japan's interest payments to 4% of GDP and push its fiscal deficit, the shortfall in government revenue compared to government expenses, to 11% of GDP from the recent 7%. Writes Feldstein:

> Higher deficits, moreover, would cause the ratio of debt to GDP to rise from its already high level, which implies greater debt-service costs and, therefore, even larger deficits. This vicious spiral of rising deficits and debt would be likely to push interest rates even higher, causing the spiral to accelerate.
>
> The larger deficits would also eliminate all of the excess saving that now underpins the current-account surplus. The same negative effect on the current account could occur if the corporate sector increases its rate of investment in plant and equipment or reduces corporate saving by paying higher wages or dividends. The excess saving could also decline if housing construction picks up.[19]

---

[18] Martin Feldstein, "Japan's Saving Crisis," Project Syndicate, 24 September 2010, found at: http://www.project-syndicate.org/commentary/feldstein28/English, accessed 2 November 2011.

[19] Ibid.

Japan would have its day of reckoning and the impact would be felt throughout the global economy.

Japan's Rocky Road

In three decades, Japan has gone from an economic juggernaut to economic laggard. Its attempts to revive its economy through the use of both monetary and fiscal policy — although generally ineffective — have left the country with the largest debt-to-GDP ratio of any developed nation in modern history.

For a time, Japan was able to fund its large government debt internally because of historically high household savings, but those days have come to an end. A small change from the mild deflation that has characterized Japan's economy for the past decade to mild inflation will cause the government's debt to grow much more quickly than the pool of savings available to fund it. The government of Japan would have to borrow large amounts internationally at potentially high costs. The results would be disastrous for Japan and the developed world.

What Can You Do to Recover?

- Be wary of bubbles. Most bubbles are created, at least in part, by excessive investment in real estate, which is funded by easily available bank credit and facilitated by low interest rates. This has been the case in the United States, Britain and much of Europe.
- Japan is an excellent case study for what happens when bubbles burst. As market participants attempt to reduce their debt or deleverage, economic growth slows dramatically. This is often referred to as a balance sheet recession, as it is caused by businesses and households trying to repair their balance sheets by reducing spending. This is happening throughout Europe and the United States.
- When fiscal stimulus is withdrawn too soon, the country can be forced back into recession. This is a significant danger in the United States.
- Too much government austerity can make the downturn worse, as a vicious cycle of falling economic activity leads to reduced tax revenues and higher transfer payments, which leads to ever larger deficits and even lower economic activity.
- Japan poses a significant threat to global financial stability should it face a funding issue with its massive government debt.

CHAPTER 6

China:
Saviour of the World?

IN NOVEMBER 2008, China stepped up to the plate and hit one out of the park. It introduced a massive, 4-trillion-yuan or US$586-billion stimulus package — 14% of its GDP — that became the play of the game. China's economy rebounded and China went to the top of the standings.

In the process, China gave the world economy a much-needed boost. Its appetite for resources benefitted commodities-driven countries such as Canada and Australia; its rising consumer class created demand for domestic and Western goods; and, its accumulation of US$1.2 trillion in U.S. debt helped to backstop the U.S. economy.

Perhaps, China is the saviour of the world.

But really, only people looking for simple solutions believe that. The reality is a lot more complicated. Although China has accomplished an astonishing economic and political turnaround in recent decades, becoming the world's second largest economy behind only the United States, it has done so at a price. And the nagging concern is that behind closed doors, China's banks have stock-piled bad loans and its booming real estate market has produced empty houses.

What if the unintended consequence of China's stimulus program is a bubble large enough that, if it bursts, it will shatter the global economy? Saviour or risk to our future stability? No one knows. There is, however, compelling evidence that China's ability to lead a sustained recovery is limited. Taken together, they provide a cautionary tale for those with an overly optimistic view of China's capabilities.

China's Glorious Past

For many centuries, China and India were dominant players in a much smaller world economy. Noted economic historian Angus Maddison reconstructed the GDP of the world's economy back to 1 A.D. He found that by virtue of both population and innovation, China and India led the world for most of the past 2,000 years.[1]

For example, in 1000, China's GDP was about 2.5 times that of Western Europe. By 1500, it was 1.5 times that of Western Europe. The gap then narrowed so that by 1700, the GDPs of China and Europe were roughly equal. But then, Maddison reports, China's GDP grew much faster than that of Europe for the next 120 years, so that by 1820, China once again had a GDP roughly 40% larger than that of Western Europe.

It was only when the Industrial Revolution took hold in Western Europe that China's dominant place in the world's economy began to slip. By 1870, Western Europe's GDP was roughly twice that of China's. China's self-imposed isolation from the rest of the world opened that gap wider. By 1973, China's GDP was only 20% of Western Europe's GDP. After the 1976 death of Mao Zedong, Deng Xiaoping assumed power and China began its return to greatness, affecting an economic transformation perhaps unprecedented in world history. By 2003, on the basis of purchasing power parity, China's GDP had grown to 80% of that of Western Europe, boasting an average annual compound growth rate of 7.3%, versus 2.2% in Western Europe. China, the renewed economic powerhouse, had arrived.

The Cultural Revolution

Politically, the years leading up to 1949 and the People's Republic were unsettled, according to China scholar Wang Jisi in a paper entitled "China's Search for a Grand Strategy: A Rising Great Power Finds Its Way." Jisi notes:

> From ancient times, the ruling regime of the day has often been brought down by a combination of internal uprising and external invasion. The Ming dynasty collapsed in 1644 after rebelling peasants took the capital city of Beijing and the Manchu, with the collusion of Ming generals, invaded from the north. Some three centuries later, the Manchu's own Qing dynasty collapsed after a series of internal revolts coincided with invasions by Western and Japanese forces. The end of the Kuomintang's rule

---

[1] Angus Maddison, *Contours of the World Economy, 1–2003 AD: Essays in Macroeconomic History* (New York: Oxford University Press, 2007). All GDP numbers in these paragraph are Maddison's.

and founding of the People's Republic in 1949 was caused by an indigenous revolution inspired and then bolstered by the Soviet Union and the International Movement.[2]

In 1949, the Communists under Mao Zedong established an autocratic socialist system that, although ensuring China's sovereignty, imposed strict controls over everyday life. The Great Proletarian Cultural Revolution of 1966 to 1976, more commonly known as the "Cultural Revolution," moved to banish capitalist and bourgeois elements from Chinese society. It led to the displacement of large swaths of China's urban population, with millions of urban youth forcibly sent to the countryside. Property was seized and historical relics and artefacts were destroyed. Deng Xiaoping, soon to become the leader who would lead China toward a more enlightened future, was himself a victim of the Cultural Revolution's movement to root out capitalist sympathizers. During Mao Zedong's tenure, tens of millions of lives were lost.

After Mao Zedong died in 1976, Deng Xiaoping returned to power and began the transformation of China from impoverished nation to economic power by unshackling China's economy. The Chinese public responded to the economic liberalism with enthusiasm, although the Communist Party kept a tight rein on the political levers of power.

Today, China has both military and economic power and it wants the world to grasp its ascendancy. During the American debt crisis, for example, China used its position as the holder of US$1.2 trillion in U.S. debt to admonish the U.S., telling the ailing giant to get its fiscal house in order. In a statement released through the state-run Xinhua News Agency, it warned:

> The U.S. Government has to come to terms with the painful fact that the good old days when it could just borrow its way out of messes of its own making are finally gone. China, the largest creditor of the world's sole superpower has every right now to demand the United States address its structural debt problems and ensure the safety of China's dollar assets.

China seems determined to play a stronger political and economic role on the world stage than in the recent past.

It is in our best interests to read the signs and relate them to our economy.

---

[2] Wang Jisi, "China's Search for a Grand Strategy: A Rising Great Power Finds Its Way," *Foreign Affairs Magazine* (March/April 2011).

Murky Waters

Getting a handle on China's economic policies, however, is challenging at best. Although China's foreign and defense strategies appear well developed and defined, the same cannot be said for its economic policies. In fact, several factors make getting a clear picture of China's economy a nearly impossible task. First on the list would be the way the country operates.

Most countries operate on one of two systems, maintains William Gamble, a Newport, Rhode Island-based lawyer who specializes in emerging markets. In a rules-based system, codified laws govern most activities. In a relationship-based system, relationships govern much of a country's operations, making bribes all-important. Explains Gamble: "The reason you do a bribe is that it establishes the relationship and relationships are very important."

As a result, relationship-based systems are hotbeds of "crony capitalism" in which connections among governments, state-owned firms and large family firms create a convenient, self-serving triangle. "These firms dominate these economies," Gamble says, "and because they can write the laws and because they know to whom to talk, they stifle the competition." This also leads to a lack of accurate information since the three sides of the triangle make as little information as possible public.

China falls into this latter category.

According to Gamble, who applies concepts from law and economics to the legal infrastructure of countries to determine the efficiency of their markets, the law does not work well in China. So, the individual's ability to get things done depends on connections, preferably family connections. About 70% of the Chinese firms listed on the Hong Kong Stock Exchange are still operated day to day by the firm's founder or descendants. "If you're related within that firm, you know whom to contact," he says. "This has enormous implications. It's one of the main reasons why we in the West don't get it."

Another factor, the numbers and forecasts that come from these restricted sources — whose jobs depend on optimistic reports — tend to be suspect. This all makes Western principles of economic analysis redundant because the numbers upon which the analysis is based may be faulty.

Further muddying the waters, demand in China is often distorted by government control of the marketplace. Gamble sites copper as an example. Large orders of copper lead to the belief that industrialization is proceeding at a great pace. That is not the case. Copper is put to an unusual use; it is often stored and used as bank collateral. Because land is owned by the government, it cannot be used as collateral. These and other indications mean that the "boom" in China may not be as great as believed in the West.

Finally, there is a huge underground economy. Best estimates put it at 50% of China's US$14-trillion economy. Getting a handle on China's true economic power is difficult indeed.

China's Credit Explosion

As a part of its stimulus program, China pumped 21.3 trillion yuan into its banking system over three years: 9.6 trillion yuan in 2009, 7.97 yuan trillion in 2010 and 3.75 trillion yuan in 2011. It was a massive injection of capital into the economy, in fact, more than thirty-six times pre-recession amounts.

Much of China's credit explosion found its way into the country's state-owned businesses. As was their habit, state-owned banks loaned money to state-owned companies in an effort to stave off the effects of the downturn. But the People's Bank of China reported in 2011 that up to 30% of outstanding bank loans — or 14.37 trillion yuan — were made to local governments through off-balance sheet vehicles called "local-government financing platforms."[3] And that amount seems to be missing from official accounts.

A report from Moody's Investors Service Inc. in July 2011 suggested that China's National Audit Office had understated the size of potentially problematic loans by 3.5 trillion yuan or US$540 billion[4] because it had not taken loans to local governments fully into account. Moody's estimated a delinquency rate of 50% to 75% on local government loans, raising the spectre that the Chinese banking system's non-performing loans could reach 8% to 12% of total loans.

The report also noted that it was unclear how the banks and authorities planned to deal with the problem. It cited the apparent absence of a clear master plan and the potential for a negative credit outlook for the country's banks.

Moody's suggested that one of three scenarios would unfold:

- The Chinese government could take a hands-off approach and leave the banks and local governments to sort out the situation. This would mean continued opacity, disputes over payments and damaged credibility for banks and regulators, leading to reduced investor confidence.

---

[3] Martin Vaughan and Aaron Back, "Moody's Warns on China Debt," *Wall Street Journal* [New York] 6 July 2011, found at: http://online.wsj.com/article/SB10001424052702304803104576427062691548064.html, accessed 20 November 2011.

[4] Report on China's debt, Moody's Investors Service, Inc., 5 July 2011.

- The Chinese government could provide financial assistance to local governments and banks and remove toxic loans from their balance sheets. That would limit banks' losses but act as a disincentive on future loans and erode investor confidence.
- A gradual tightening of lending guidelines, ensuring more secure future sources of repayment. Some existing loans would be restructured. However, the ability of the banks to absorb losses out of current earnings would be reliant upon continued strong growth in earnings.

Moody's saw the last scenario as the most likely.

It is also possible China's credit explosion only exacerbated an already-difficult situation. Gamble believes China's state-owned banks were burdened with bad loans before 2009's stimulus package upped the ante. State-owned businesses, he maintains, often don't replay loans and banks have bad loans on their books going back to 2001. Banks have exchanged those loans for company bonds bearing the face value of the loans and transferred the bonds to asset management companies. The plan was to sell the bonds and recoup the losses. But that hasn't happened.

So, that is risk Number One in China — the impact that trillions of yuan of loans that may never be repaid could have on China's banking system.

Real Estate Bubble?

The closed banking system and government policies of intervention in the marketplace have contributed to the serious misallocation of capital, first through the banking system but also in real estate. China has been building apartments buildings in which no one lives.

In a typical scenario, the government evicts peasants from the land and sells the land to developers. The developers get cheap loans from banks to build apartments. However, Gamble says, the apartments are too high-priced for local residents who cannot obtain mortgages. The housing sits there empty, while the hundreds of millions of rural Chinese who have migrated to cities have nowhere to live.

Some estimates placed the number of unsold apartments at more than 64 million as of mid-2011.

In essence, China is building large ghost towns in many areas of the country, including Beijing.

This raises many issues, not least of which may be a bad-debt problem that heightens the risk of default, exerting a serious drag on China's economic growth. Bigger still, if there is a housing bubble — and it bursts — the damage will extend beyond China and threaten our fragile global economy. China's status as the world's second largest economy means that whatever transpires there will be felt around the world.

What Can You Do to Recover?

- Be ready for a drop in demand for Canadian commodities, as China sorts out its economic issues. That will lower commodities prices and put a damper not only on Canadian companies supplying those commodities but also on Canadian economic growth. As Gamble puts it: "Don't bet the farm" on continued high commodity sales.
- Reduce your risk by avoiding mutual funds with heavy weightings in China. Opt for global funds in which China has a small weighting.
- Be ready financially and emotionally for more market volatility and economic uncertainty. Don't be thrown by more turbulence — you suspected it was coming and it isn't unexpected. And make sure your financial house is in order so you can weather any new storms.

CHAPTER 7

Canada:
An Endangered Species

IN CANADA, WE PRIDE OURSELVES on having weathered the global downturn relatively well. Sure, we dipped into recession for a couple of quarters but our federal government, debt under control, back-stopped our bankers and initiated a much-needed infrastructure spending program. So, we're feeling pretty secure. Canada with its clean air, clean water, safe cities and — fairly — solid economy truly is an oasis in a less-than-perfect world.

But should we be so unconcerned? Are we really that much better off than our neighbour to the south? If we take a look at several metrics comparing Canada and the United States, what will the data tell us? More important, what does the data mean from a portfolio-planning perspective? How should we interpret the data to best position ourselves in the months and years ahead? Whether you are a thirty-something on the fast track to the C-suite or a retiree living on a fixed income, getting a good read on Canada's economy is critical to your financial well-being.

Canada's Banks: Some of the Best in the World?
Let's begin by looking at the banking sectors in Canada and the United States, because failures in the banking sector were where it all started. Canada has what is referred to as a "branch" banking system; the U.S. historically has had primarily a "unit" banking system, although in recent years it has been moving toward a form of branch banking. This essential difference in structure and history has produced very different types of banks with different risk profiles.

There are three categories of banks in Canada: Schedule I, Schedule II and Schedule III. Schedule I banks are domestic banks that are authorized under the federal *Bank Act* to accept deposits and which may be eligible for deposit insurance provided by the Canadian Deposit Insurance Corporation (CDIC). Schedule II banks are foreign bank subsidiaries that are allowed to accept deposits and make loans in Canada. Schedule III banks operate in Canada as branches of foreign banks. As of late summer 2011, there were twenty-two Schedule I banks, twenty-five Schedule II banks and twenty-nine Schedule III banks authorized by the Office of the Superintendent of Financial Institutions (OSFI), the federal entity that regulates banks, to conduct banking in Canada.[1] That makes a total of seventy-six banks operating in Canada, an unusually high number indicating the growth the sector has enjoyed in the past decade or so. As recently as September 1998, when the Task Force on the Future of the Canadian Financial Services Sector released its report, known as the "MacKay Report," there were only fifty-four banks in Canada — forty-six foreign banks and eight domestic banks.

Canada has a history of few banks and even fewer bank failures. Since 1923, only three banks have failed in Canada, the Home Bank of Canada in August 1923 and the Canadian Commercial Bank (CCB) and Northland Bank both in September 1985. CCB and Northland were relatively young banks, having received their bank charters in 1974 and 1975, respectively. Both were Alberta-based regional banks that grew quickly through the boom years of the 1970s, lending heavily to the real estate and oil and gas sectors in Western Canada. When the Canadian economy collapsed in the early 1980s under the strain of historically high interest rates, the two regional banks were too narrowly focused on both sides of their balance sheets to survive.

(As an aside, that is not to say Canada's banks have been universally admired within its own borders. There has always been a sense that Western rural constituents weren't well served by the Eastern-based big banks. Witness the births of both CCB and Northland Bank. They had a precedent in successfully run Alberta Treasury Branches (ATB), established in 1938 by then-Alberta Premier William Aberhart. Aberhart was concerned that the Eastern banks would accept deposits in rural Western Canada, then lend these funds in the urban areas of Central Canada where they could earn a higher rate of return. Albertans would be left without the credit they needed. To counter this perceived threat, he set up the ATB as a uniquely Alberta-based financial institution, which still operates as an Alberta Crown Corporation under the name ATB Financial.)

---

[1] A complete list of Canadian banks can be found on the Office of the Superintendent of Financial Institutions website: www.osfi-bsif.gc.ca/osfi/index_e.aspx?DetailID=568 or the website of the Canadian Bankers Association: www.cba.ca/en/banks-in-canada.

Still, the Canadian way of a small number of relatively large banks with many branches has served us well. Their extensive branch networks have allowed the banks to gather large amounts of "sticky" retail deposits from across the country, which they then move internally to where it is needed. This focus on retail deposits has reduced the need for the banks to go to the money markets to fund their loan portfolios, thereby making the banks, in large part, immune to a "run" on the bank.[2] Spreading their business across Canada also lets the large banks diversify their loan portfolios both geographically and by sector, which reduces the risk that problems within any one sector or area will bring down the bank, as happened with CCB and Northland Bank.

U.S. Distrust of Large Banks

The banking system in the United States is highly fragmented, with many more banks and more bank failures than Canada. The U.S. banking system evolved from a deep distrust of large banks and the economic power that they could wield. In fact, Thomas Jefferson, the third president of the United States had the following to say about banks:

> I believe that banking institutions are more dangerous to our liberties than standing armies. If the American people ever allow private banks to control the issue of their currency, first by inflation, then by deflation, the banks and corporations that will grow up around [the banks] will deprive the people of all property until their children wake-up homeless on the continent their fathers conquered. The issuing power should be taken from the banks and restored to the people, to whom it properly belongs.[3]

Jefferson believed even more strongly than Alberta's Aberhart that big banks are bad for society. Jefferson worked hard to ensure that no large bank could exist in the U.S. This led in many states to the aptly named "unit" banking system, whereby a bank was not allowed to branch, either within the state or between states. The result was a very large number of one-office banks. For example, when the Continental Illinois Bank failed in 1984, it was the seventh largest bank in the U.S. with about US$40 billion in assets. It had one location, in Chicago.

---

[2] In general, deposits up to $100,000 are covered by deposit insurance offered by Canada Deposit Insurance Corporation (CDIC). Because small investors know that their deposits are protected in the event of a bank failure, they are much less inclined to pull their deposits in the face of risk than are money-market lenders, who are not covered by CDIC insurance for the bulk of their deposits.

[3] The Quotations Page found at: http://www.quotationspage.com/quote/37700.html, accessed 27 October 2011.

This lack of a branch network made the U.S. banks vulnerable to two risks, one from the left-hand side of the balance sheet and the other from the right-hand side. First, because most banks were physically located in a small number of locations, it was hard to grow the bank's assets quickly. (In banking, a loan is considered an asset because the bank only lends the money; a deposit is a liability because the bank owes the depositor his or her money.) So, banks would buy loan portfolios. Continental Illinois bought a large portfolio of energy loans from Penn Square Bank, an Oklahoma-based bank — which is what led to Continental Illinois's eventual failure. Continental Illinois failed to examine carefully the quality of the loans it was buying and, as often happens when we don't pay proper attention to the business at hand, it paid the ultimate price.

The second problem arises on the funding side of the bank. Without a large branch network to gather retail deposits, a large U.S. bank has no choice but to fund its loans in the money market. Money market funding is often referred to as "hot money" because it will flee at the first whiff of trouble. This is exactly what happened with Continental Illinois. When the repayment of the energy loans it had purchased began to fail at an ever-increasing rate, money market investors pulled their funds. It was like a game of musical chairs, with nobody wanting to be the person left standing when the music stopped. It was a classic run on the bank and it did not take long for the bank to fail.

In the roaring 1920s, the number of banks in the U.S. peaked at about 30,000.[4] The next decade was extremely hard on the U.S. banking system: about 9,000 banks failed in the 1930s with about 4,000 of them failing in 1933 alone.[5] By 1984, the number of commercial banks in the U.S. was 14,496, which steadily declined thereafter, so that by the end of 2010, there were only 6,529 commercial banks left in the U.S.[6] As of September 8, 2011, that number had shrunk further, to 6,368 U.S. banks and 1,085 savings institutions insured by the Federal Deposit Insurance Corporation (FDIC).[7] The bank failures were mounting up. In the first nine months of 2011, there were seventy bank failures, on top of 157 bank failures in 2010, 140 in 2009

---

[4] "Banking in the United States," *Encyclopedia Americana* (Grolier online) found at: http://teacher.scholastic.com/scholasticnews/indepth/upfront/grolier/Banking.htm, accessed 27 October 2011.

[5] Bill Ganzel, "Farming in the 1930s," *Wessels Living History Farm* (York, Nebraska) 2003, found at: http://www.livinghistoryfarm.org/farminginthe30s/money_08.html, accessed 27 October 2011.

[6] "Historcial Statistics for banking," Federal Deposit Insurance Corporation, found at: http://www2.fdic.gov/hsob/index.asp, accessed 27 October 2011.

[7] Ibid.

and twenty-five in 2008. In the year preceding the global downturn, 2007, there had been just three failures.[8] No U.S. banks failed in 2005 and 2006.

From 1934, when the FDIC was created, until September 2011, there were 3,356 bank failures in the U.S., compared to just two bank failures in Canada in the same period.

The inability to branch created a U.S. banking system that was highly vulnerable to local shocks. When a region or industry ran into economic trouble, the banks that served that region or industry could not help but be dragged down as well.

Innovation and Securitization

There is a bright side, however. The regulatory structure that prevented branching led the U.S. banks to greater innovation, one of which was the use of "securitization" to manage their balance sheets. To securitize, a bank would pool a number of loans — generally mortgages — of differing durations and rates and package them into a security. It would then sell shares in that security to a number of investors. When the bank sold the mortgages, it would get back cash that it could use to make new loans.

Take the example of a small bank in a fast-growing, sun-belt state. Typically, demand for new mortgage loans would be higher than its inflow of new deposits. To manage this imbalance, the bank would securitize its mortgages, thereby allowing it to make new loans without growing the size of its balance sheet. This accomplished some of the benefits of a large branch system without actually having to build a large branch system.

In the early 1980s, however, the U.S. began to dismantle many of the laws and regulations that had shaped its banking sector, leading to a wave of bank consolidation that has continued to this day. Yet, most large U.S. banks still make extensive use of "wholesale" funding, as their branch networks are not yet large enough to fund the growth in the asset side of their balance sheets.

This combination of a reliance on money-market funding to feed the right-hand side of the balance sheet and poor asset quality on the left-hand side of the balance sheet proved fatal for most of the large U.S. banks, as the default rate of subprime loans escalated throughout the spring, summer and fall of 2008.

---

[8] "Bank Failures in Brief," Federal Deposit Insurance Corporation, found at: http://www.fdic. gov/bank/historical/bank/2008/index.html, accessed 27 October 2011.

So How Do We Measure Up?

What impact has this history had on the performance of the two countries' banking sectors in the dark days since 2008? Let's take as our guide the common share prices of four major banks, two Canadian and two U.S., for the five years ended September 2011. Although two banks certainly do not make a banking system, the banks chosen here are reasonable proxies for the fortunes of the sector. From Canada we have Royal Bank of Canada (RBC) and Bank of Montreal (BMO); representing the U.S. banking sector are Bank of America (BofA) and Citigroup (Citi).

Now to performance: let's look at each of the banks in turn, paying attention to the relative loss of market capitalization (or market "cap," the number of shares outstanding multiplied by the price per share) from their cyclical highs, through the downturn to the recovery leading up to September 2011. We'll start with the two Canadian banks, then turn to the two U.S. banks.

Royal Bank of Canada. In the fall of 2007, a common share of RBC was trading in the C$55-C$58 range.[9] By mid-February 2009, the share price had dropped to $21.65; in sixteen months it had lost 62% of its value. Then it bounced back, reaching a new high of $61.73 in mid-April 2010, before settling in the fall of 2011 at $47.66, roughly $2 less than its price in September 2006. Although no one likes to experience this kind of volatility, an investor who stayed the course saw the value of his or her holding decrease by about 4% over the five-year period, a loss RBC dividends would have gone a long way toward mitigating.[10]

Bank of Montreal. BMO shares exhibited a similar pattern, although with less of a bounce back. In mid-February 2007, BMO reached a five-year high of $72.15 a share. Like RBC, two years later it had sunk — in this case to a low of $24.66 a share the week of February 16, 2009. By April 2010, it was back trading pretty consistently in the $60-range. BMO ended the five-year period at $58.60 a share, $8.37 less than it started it in September 2006. The wealth of the BMO shareholder who stayed the course for the five-year period decreased by 12.5%, excluding dividends.[11]

---

[9] Share prices for RBC and BMO common shares can be found on the TMX website: www. tmx.quotemedia.com. All share price information is quoted in Canadian dollars.

[10] "Dividend History of Common Shares," Royal Bank of Canada Investor Relations, found at http://www.rbc.com/investorrelations/ir_dividend_common.html, accessed 27 October 2011. For the five-year period above RBC dividends held steady, and in some quarters increased.

[11] "Dividend information," BMO Financial Group, found at http://www.bmo.com/home/ about/banking/investor-relations/shareholder-information/dividend-information#C2, accessed 27 October 2010. In the five years, BMO dividends held steady.

Although the five-year price performance of the two Canadian banks was not great, it is much, much better than that experienced by our two U.S. examples. Citi, in fact, had a near-death experience, and BofA was not far behind.

Citigroup. A Citi common share began the period at a price of US$49.50 and reached a peak of $55.70 in December 2006.[12] The shares then took a long, precipitous slide that ended with a price of $1.03 a share the week of March 9, 2009 — a loss of 98% of its market value. The price of Citi stock dropped so low, and remained there for so long, that on March 21, 2011, the bank announced a share consolidation, giving each shareholder one new share for ten old shares. The effect was to boost the value of Citi shares to about ten times its previous level.

Was this a good move for Citi shareholders? Only time will tell, but a 2008 study of stock consolidations, also known as "reverse stock splits," found that the typical stock underperformed the broad market by 50% on a risk-adjusted basis for the three-year period after the reverse split occurred.[13] As author Jim Rosenfeld, an associate professor of finance at Emory University's Goizueta Business School in Atlanta, Georgia, told *Bloomberg Businessweek* magazine: "Reverse stock splits are a strong indicator that the company is going to be a significant underperformer during the near future."[14]

Bank of America. BofA shareholders have suffered almost as badly as those of Citigroup — but only almost. In September 2006, the beginning of the period, BofA's share price was $52.43. That November, it peaked at $54.85 before beginning a long, choppy fall to a low of $3.14 the week of March 2, 2009 — a 94% drop in market value. BofA stock then recovered marginally, ending the period at a value of $6.98 a share, still down 87% from its five-year high.

Canada Comes Out Ahead?

Are Canadian banks truly that much better managed than their American counterparts? The short answer would be "Yes."

---

[12] Share price information for Citi and BofA can be found on Yahoo Finance at: http://ca.finance.yahoo.com. All share price information for the two banks are in U.S. dollars.

[13] Seoyoung Kim, April Klein and James Rosenfeld, "Return Performance Surrounding Reverse Stock Splits: Can Investors Profit?" *Financial Management* 37 issue 2 (Summer, 2008) pp. 173-192.

[14] Lauren Young, "Is Citigroup's Reverse Stock Split a Smart Move?" *Bloomberg Businessweek*, 19 March 2009, found at: http://www.businessweek.com/investing/insights/blog/archives/2009/03/why_citis_rever.html, accessed 27 October 2011.

The relatively strong performance of the Canadian banking sector, as exemplified by the stock of Royal Bank of Canada and Bank of Montreal, is a reflection of fundamentally stronger balance sheets.

But there was an element of luck. Canadian banks were late to the real estate party enjoyed by their American counterparts. Federal regulations had prevented Canadian banks from moving into the most risky sectors of the residential lending market, the subprime market, as their American counterparts had done. But Canadian banks were definitely moving in that direction. Beginning in the first half of the 2000s, maximum mortgage amortization periods in Canada moved quickly to forty years from twenty-five and minimum down payments on homes went from 10% to zero.

Had the housing downturn not occurred when it did but a few years later, the story might have ended differently for Canadian banks. As it turned out, Canadian banks dodged a bullet. In early 2010, the Canadian government moved quickly to rein in the weakening of minimum lending standards.[15]

Debt and Taxes: How Do We Compare?

Today, when it comes to government debt and government spending, Canada is often held up as a model of virtue in a not so virtuous world.

Indeed, Canada has come a long way. In the early 1990s, Canada was considered an economic basket case. It had reached such a point that, in January 1995, the *Wall Street Journal* ran an editorial suggesting that Canada had become an honorary member of the Third World and, like Britain in the 1970s or New Zealand in the 1980s, might need to call in the International Monetary Fund (IMF) to stabilize its falling currency.[16] As an indication of a government spending far more than it received in tax revenue, federal government debt as a percentage of gross domestic product (GDP) had risen steadily for twenty years, from a low of 18.4% in 1974-75 to a high of 68.4% in 1995-96, the highest since the post-war years of 1948-49.[17] Government after government had run large deficits and Canada was close to the danger

---

[15] On February 16, 2010, the federal Department of Finance announced a number of mea-sures to support the long-term stability of the Canadian housing market. The new rules, which took effect April 16, 2010, for government- insured mortgages are:
   a. All borrowers must meet the standards for a five-year fixed-rate term mortgage;
   b. The maximum amount on which a mortgage can be refinanced is 90% of home value;
   c. Non-owner occupied homes require a 20% down payment.
   The full text of the release can be found at: http://www.fin.gc.ca/n10/10-011-eng.asp.

[16] "Bankrupt Canada?" *Wall Street Journal*, 12 January1995, page A14.

[17] Marc-Andre Pigeon, "The Debt-to-GDP Target: Options and Considerations," Parliamen-tary Information and Research Service, 11 May 2005.

zone. When provincial government debts were combined with federal debts, Canada's debt-to-GDP ratio was second only to Italy among the members of the Organization for Economic Cooperation and Development (OECD).

Canada began the long road back to fiscal health in the 1996-97 fiscal year, when then-Finance Minister Paul Martin cut federal program spending by 8.7%. Over the years, the deficit turned into a surplus, and the government gradually paid down its outstanding debt. By 2008, at the start of the current crisis, Canada's federal debt had fallen to 29% of GDP, a result of both a growing economy and a 17% reduction in debt, to $464 billion from $562 billion in 1997.

Because of the federal government's long period of fiscal prudence, when the crises of 2008 erupted, Canada had much more fiscal room to manoeuvre than did its counterparts in the OECD. As a result, Canada is often held out as a role model for other countries to emulate.

So, just how do we stack up against our monolithic neighbour to the south?

According to the OECD's *Government at a Glance 2011* publication, the United States government debt was 94% of GDP in 2010 whereas Canada's was 84%.[18]

How can this be? How could the Canadian government debt-to-GDP ratio go from 29% in 2008 to 84% in 2010? The answer lies in the calculation of the numerator, the debt. The OECD calculates the debt of all levels of government, not just the federal government. Canada's federal government has done an excellent job of managing its debt, so that in 2010 the federal government's debt-to-GDP ratio was just 37%, but the provinces have been running up debt, giving Canada a total government debt-to-GDP ratio of 84%.

It is not just federal government debt that matters — all debt matters.

William Watson, economics professor at McGill University in Montreal, put it this way in the *National Post*:

Of course, the Americans are digging their debt hole deeper at a faster rate than we are. Their deficit-to-GDP ratio is 10.6% while ours is only 5.5%. Part of the deficit is cyclical and will go away when the economy recovers. Even so, the OECD calculates Canada

---

[18] Organization for Economic Cooperation and Development, *Government at a Glance 2011* (Paris, 2011), p.83.

has a structural deficit of 3.7% of GDP — that is, a deficit that would still be there even if we were at full employment.

The usual view among Canadian intelligentsia is that the United States will have to cut its deficit not by cutting spending but by raising revenue. Is that true? If you look at how much U.S. governments spend per person, the total is $19,266. How much does government spend on each Canadian? $16,655. Less? The Tea Party could hack away $10,000 of spending per American family of four and U.S. governments would still be spending more per person than governments in Canada.

Should the U.S. raise taxes instead? The average American is already spending $14,154 in taxes, which is only $415 less than the average Canadian. If Canadians are overtaxed, maybe they're overtaxed, too.[19]

What conclusions can we draw from the OECD data and Watson's comments? How well does Canada stack up against its neighbour to the south? It seems Canada is not doing nearly as well as Canadians believe. On a consolidated basis, Canada has far more debt than is commonly thought, the Canadian government spends less per citizen than the U.S. government and Canadians pay slightly more in taxes than Americans do. From an investment and planning perspective, Canada's debt levels will soon dampen future expectations of growth — and that's a problem.

Back to "Bad" Debt

Let's go back to the Bank for International Settlements (BIS) paper we discussed in Chapter 2 which posited that once central government debt reaches 85% of GDP, it is indeed a drag on growth.[20] The OECD puts Canada's total government debt-to-GDP ratio at 84%. This is alarmingly close to the 85% threshold identified by the BIS authors.

But the BIS authors don't stop at government debt: "Our examination of other types of debt yields similar conclusions. When corporate debt goes beyond 90% of GDP, it becomes a drag on growth. And for household debt, we report a threshold around 85% of GDP, although the impact is very imprecisely estimated."

So, if we add up the three thresholds of government (85%), corporate (90%) and household (85%), we obtain a total threshold of 260%. What is the relative state of these three debts between Canada and the United States?

[19] William Watson, "As Triple A as we Think," *National Post*, 9 September 2011, p. FP11.
[20] Stephen G. Cecchetti, M.S. Mohanty and Fabrizio Zampolli, "The real effects of debt," *Bank for International Settlements Working Papers* No. 352 (September 2011).

The following table presents a not-so-rosy picture. It shows that Canada's total debt-to-GDP ratio is 313%, versus only 268% for the United States. Given that Canada's government debt-to-GDP ratio is slightly below that of the U.S., it suggests that *Canada's household and corporate debts are higher as a percentage of GDP than are those in the U.S.*

Household, Corporate and Government Debt as a Percentage of Nominal GDP

	Levels				Changes**		
	1980	1990	2000	2010*	1980-90	1990-2000	2000-10
United States	151	200	198	268	49	-2	70
Japan	290	364	410	456	75	46	46
Germany	136	137	226	241	1	89	15
United Kingdom	160	203	223	322	43	20	99
France	160	198	243	321	37	45	78
Italy	109	180	252	310	71	72	58
Canada	236	278	293	313	42	15	20
Australia	128	174	185	235	46	11	49
Austria	162	178	205	238	16	27	32
Belgium	170	264	298	356	94	34	58
Denmark			259	336			77
Finland	146	173	222	270	26	49	48
Greece	92	139	195	262	47	55	67
Netherlands	205	265	294	327	60	29	33
Norway			256	334			78
Portugal	144	141	251	366	-2	110	115
Spain	172	187	258	355	15	70	97
Sweden	219	289	320	340	70	31	21
Total of above							
Median	160	192	251	322	45	40	58
Weighted average***	172	218	246	306	47	28	61
Simple average	168	211	255	314	43	44	59
G7	177	223	264	303	45	41	55
Other advanced	160	201	249	321	41	46	61
Memo: Std deviation	50	64	54	43			

* Some figures refer to 2009.

** In percentage points of GDP.

*** Based on 2005 GDP and PPP exchange rates.

Source: *Bank for International Settlements*

That is not good news. When Canadian consumers stop spending and start saving in order to pay down debts, the impact will be felt immediately. When a household spends money at the mall, goes out for dinner or buys a new car, the impact is a virtuous circle felt throughout the economy. Retailers buy more inventory, restaurants hire more workers, workers get more overtime. As workers make more money, they spend more and as workers spend more, employers hire more — it's a self-reinforcing cycle.

Unfortunately, it also works the other way around. When households reduce or stop spending, the cycle becomes self-reinforcing in the opposite direction. As consumers spend less, employers hire less, workers make less — which means even less money for spending and debt reduction. What was once a virtuous cycle upward has become a vicious cycle downward. The virtuous cycle can only begin anew when debt has been reduced to more manageable levels.

Measuring by the Head

So, it appears we need to rethink our perception of debt — it is, indeed, as big a risk in Canada as in the U.S., maybe bigger. That begs the question: are there other areas of the Canadian economy that present additional risk to our fragile recovery? Let's look at "per capita" indicators to get a fix on the impact of the downturn on Canadians' and Americans' wealth.

Net worth per capita. Generally, per capita net worth in Canada and the U.S. moved in sync, trending upward — until June 2006, that is, when the overheated U.S. housing market exploded. Per capita net worth in the U.S. fell immediately and steeply; in Canada the net worth per capita continued upward, correcting in early 2008 before resuming its upward trajectory — opening an ever-widening gap between Canadian and U.S. per capita net worth. By mid-2011, Canada's net worth per capita was $186,900[21] while the U.S. net worth per capita was nudging toward $150,000.[22] Behind the precipitous fall in U.S. per capita net worth was the destruction of wealth associated with residential real estate.

Real per capita assets: housing and real per capita housing equity. This destruction of real estate wealth becomes abundantly clear by looking at two other metrics: real per capita assets: housing and real per capita housing equity. The former is the per capita value of residential housing,

---

[21] National Balance Sheet Accounts, Statistics Canada, 13 September 2001, found at http://www.statcan.gc.ca/daily-quotidien/110913/dq110913a-eng.htm, accessed 28 October 2011.

[22] Stephen Gordon, Mainly Canadian Economic Blog, 21 June 2011, found at : http://worthwhile.typepad.com/worthwhile_canadian_initi/2011/06/balance-sheet.html#more, accessed 28 October 2011. All per capita comparisons come from Gordon's blog.

while the latter subtracts debt held against the housing assets to leave only the equity.

Beginning in 1998, both U.S. per capita real estate values and housing equity rose steeply — until 2006, when both jumped off a cliff. In Canada, housing and housing equity per capita, while climbing steadily, never reached the heights of the U.S. — and never experienced the depths. By early 2007, U.S. per capita housing equity dropped below Canada's, but it took almost a year for U.S. per capita house prices to fall below Canadian house prices. Here, too, the gap has widened in recent years as U.S. house prices continued to crumble.

Canadian residents should take this as a cautionary tale: Canada is definitely not immune to a similar fall in residential real estate prices.

Real per capita liabilities. In the early 1990s, Canadians and Americans were roughly equally in debt, as measured by real per capita liabilities. Starting in 1995, however, Americans began ramping up their debt and outspending Canadians. This trend accelerated throughout the early 2000s, as U.S. housing values boomed. But, in 2008, Americans began to reduce their per capita liabilities while Canadians continued to add to theirs. In this case, the gap is slight, but today Canadian households definitely have more debt than their American counterparts.

Real per capita debt definitely sounds an alarm. In a world of great volatility, personal debt is an albatross; it can strangle the debtor slowly — or it can kill quickly.

Non-housing assets per capita. The pattern is the same: per capita non-housing assets in the U.S. and Canada moved more or less in sync trending steadily upward until 2003, when the pace accelerated. By 2007, however, U.S. non-housing assets per capita had sunk; a year later, Canada's dipped and recovered, once again opening a substantial gap between Canada and the U.S. non-housing assets per capita.

So, Canadians have fared relatively well during the downturn. House prices fell less than in the U.S., then recovered quickly, whereas U.S. house prices have continued to weaken. But Canadians aren't home free. Unlike Americans, Canadians have continued to take on new debt, potentially exposing the Canadian economy to a major correction when interest rates begin their climb back to more normal levels.

Global Competitiveness: Where Does Canada Rank?

What does it matter if Canada is globally competitive? Can't we just mind our own business? Not really, because being competitive is about far more than selling our products abroad; it is about prosperity. As the World Economic

Forum (WEF) defines it in *The Global Competitiveness Report 2011-2012*: "Competitiveness is the set of institutions, policies and factors that determine the level of productivity as a country. The level of productivity, in turn, sets the level of prosperity that can be earned by an economy."[23]

In its 2011-2012 report, the WEF applied its "global competitiveness index" and "twelve pillars of competitiveness" to 142 countries. As might be expected, the United States, Japan and Europe didn't fare so well. Those countries, the report says, "are experiencing slow and decelerating growth with persistent high unemployment and continued financial vulnerability."[24]

But what about Canada? It has dropped off the WEF's "Top 10" list, but only down two spots to twelfth overall. The WEF gives Canada the nod for its highly efficient markets, particularly as it relates to labour, and its well-functioning institutions and excellent infrastructure.[25] In terms of health and primary education (the fourth pillar), Canada ranks sixth; for higher education and training (the fifth pillar), it ranks twelfth. But Canada's competitiveness could be enhanced by increased research and development (R&D) spending, allowing companies to innovate and produce goods higher up the value chain. And, although Canada's banks are ranked first in the world, Canada is ranked nineteenth in terms of venture capital availability, and twenty-second in terms of ease of access to loans.

Canada's competitiveness is slipping and that raises some pressing issues. If Canada continues to lose competitiveness, every citizen will feel the impact in the form of a lower standard of living coupled with higher taxes. Canada's relatively small domestic market forces Canadian firms to look abroad for growth, but given the global malaise, Canada won't be able to export her way out of financial vulnerability any time soon. Canada's future growth will be constrained by sagging competitiveness.

What Can We Conclude About Canada?

First, Canada's banks have done remarkably well during the recent years of global turmoil. Their share prices have hung in better than many of their U.S. counterparts, in large part because of stronger balance sheets. Canadian banks' stronger balance sheets are both an accident of history — well-developed branch networks giving them access to both cheap and sticky retail deposits — and a testament to high-quality management.

---

[23] World Economic Forum, *The Global Competitiveness Report 2011-2012* (Geneva, 2011), p. 4. The report can be found at: http://www3.weforum.org/docs/WEF_GlobalCompetitivenessReport_2010-11.pdf.

[24] Ibid., p.3.

[25] Ibid., p. 25.

Will Canadian banks continue to outperform their American counterparts? The Canadian government has helped by quickly rolling back
the weaker lending standards that had crept into Canadian residential
mortgage lending prior to 2008. Will this be enough to protect the Canadian
banks should Canada's real estate market follow the path trod by the U.S.
and Europe? The answer is "Probably not" — but it will minimize the inevitable damage.

From a macro perspective, Canada may not be as strong as we like
to think. Canada's total government debt-to-GDP ratio has quickly
approached the 85% threshold at which it becomes a drag on growth. Even
though the federal government did an excellent job of reducing its debt in
decades past, less federal borrowing has been replaced with more provincial borrowing.

Granted, in the recent past, the U.S. has spent significantly more per
capita than Canada, although some portion of this would be the result of
higher military expenditures in the U.S. The result is a faster growing U.S.
deficit and higher per capita deficit in the U.S. than in Canada. And U.S.
growth is also stalling, as U.S. households begin to deleverage and get their
financial houses in order. Canadians, on the other hand, have continued to
take on more debt.

There could well be a reckoning ahead for Canada — whether it is
coming to terms with increasing government and personal debt, a bursting
real estate bubble that punctures the financial stability of the banks and
our household balance sheets, or a lower standard of living brought on
by decreasing competitiveness. The future is uncertain and our financial
recovery tenuous.

What Can You Do to Recover?

- Canada's growth will slow as high debt exerts its stranglehold on the
  future. Get ahead of the curve and reduce your personal debt now
  so that you have funds to invest when the time is right.
- The entire Western world is facing years of slow growth. Remember
  the children's story of the tortoise and the hare? As an investor,
  aspire to be the tortoise — be content to move slowly and methodi-
  cally along your chosen path toward your well-defined goal.

PART 2

Financial Recovery:
The Tools to
Make it Happen

CHAPTER 8

Fingers of Instability: Why Economic Forecasting is so Difficult

WHEN IT IS ALL LAID OUT — years of profligate spending supporting unsustainable growth — it is clear our economy is indeed fragile and that our road to financial recovery is perilous. Now, we can clearly see the need to constrain spending and restructure debt; we can accept a prolonged period of sluggish growth as the price we have to pay. But if it is all so obvious now, why wasn't it obvious in 2007, when we could have done something about it?

That is the billion-dollar question, one financial markets researchers and academics are doing their best to answer. In 2009, for example, Andrew Rose of the Haas School of Business, University of California, Berkley and Mark Spiegel from the Federal Reserve Bank of San Francisco set out to develop an "early warning system" that would alert regulators to an impending financial crisis. They reasoned that if they could identify the variables that are the precursors to an impending crisis, regulators could be forewarned and take pre-emptive action, thereby warding off a downturn. So, Rose and Spiegel looked at sixty variables across 107 countries.[1]

With such a large database covering so many countries, we almost automatically assume the researchers would succeed in their quest. Unfortunately, the actual results were much less encouraging. In the words of

---

[1] Andrew K. Rose and Mark M. Spiegel, "Cross-Country Causes and Consequences of the 2008 Crisis: Early Warning." *FRBSF Working Paper* (2009-17), found at: (www.frbsf.org/publications/economics/papers/2009/wp09-17bk.pdf), accessed 24 October 2011.

the authors: "Almost none of our posited variables are statistically signifi-cant determinants of crisis severity."[2] They later conclude: "Constructing a plausible statistical model that can predict financial crises similar to the current one will be challenging."

The experience of Rose and Spiegel suggests it is not yet possible to isolate enough variables consistently to predict an approaching financial crisis with any degree of accuracy.

So, why is forecasting the future so fiendishly difficult? If we can put a man on the moon, why can't we predict the future with a reasonable degree of accuracy? Part of the answer can be found in a book by Mark Buchanan called *Ubiquity: Why Catastrophes Happen.*[3] Buchanan is a theoretical physicist who tells a wonderful story of discovery in an engaging style.

The concepts contained in *Ubiquity* are complex. To get us started, think about your view of the world. Do you see the world as basically in equilibrium, or do you view it as chaotic and messy? Traditionally, classical economics posits that the natural state of the economy is one of equi-librium. When some external force, such as war or recession, pushes the economy away from equilibrium, it naturally returns to a state of equilib-rium over time.

But what if the natural order of things is not equilibrium but disequi-librium, or chaos and disorder? How would that change your world view? Buchanan explains it this way:

> For centuries, physicists have sought to capture the fundamental laws of the universe in timeless and unchanging equations, such as those of quantum theory or relativity. While this project has been enormously successful, the ultimate simplicity of such equations points to a paradox: if the laws of physics are so simple, why is the world so complex? Why don't ecosystems, organisms and economies reveal the same simplicity as Newton's laws and the other laws of physics?[4]

The answer, according to Buchanan, lies in the "theory of chaos" first discovered by scientists in the 1970s and 1980s. He presents the example of a pinball machine. When a pinball travels through a pinball machine, he

---

[2] Andrew K. Rose and Mark M. Spiegel, "Predicting Crises, Part II: Did Anything Matter (to Everybody)?" *FRBSF Economic Letters* (September 28, 2009).

[3] Mark Buchanan, *Ubiquity: Why Catastrophes Happen* (New York: Three Rivers Press, 2002).

[4] Ibid., p. 15.

explains, it is highly sensitive to tiny influences along the way. Each time the pinball hits a bumper, passes through a gate or is tossed by a flipper, it careens around the machine in a chaotic and unpredictable way. In a similar fashion, if a single molecule of air is somehow disturbed, it will soon disturb the molecules of air in its vicinity in random and unpredictable ways. Taken to its logical conclusion, this leads to the often-quoted "butterfly effect," which states that "the flapping of a butterfly's wings in Brazil might lead to the formation of a severe thunderstorm over Europe two weeks later."[5]

So, how do we move from butterflies to economics? Buchanan starts his story in the late 1980s with three physicists, Per Bak, Chao Tang and Kurt Weisenfeld, who were working at the Brookhaven National Laboratory in Upton, New York. Bak and his associates were trying to understand landslides and determine if there was a typical or an average size of landslides. To conduct their study, Bak and his colleagues played a simple game with a pile of sand. They randomly dropped grains of sand onto the pile. As the size of the pile grew, the sides became steeper and eventually a landslide would occur.

To their surprise, they found that there was no average size of landslide. Instead, there were a large number of very small slides and a small number of very large slides. What was predictable, however, was the relationship between size and frequency: as the size of a slide doubled, the frequency with which a slide of this size occurred decreased at a very predictable rate. This type of relationship is known as "Power Law Distribution."

But, although there was a predictable relationship between the size and the frequency of landslides, the researchers were no closer to understanding when a slide might occur or how big a slide might become once it started. Bak and his colleagues turned to their computers and some colour modelling. They imagined they were peering down on the pile of sand from above, and coloured the "sand pile" model according to its steepness. Where it was relatively flat and stable, they coloured it green; where it was steep and, in avalanche terms, ready to go, they coloured it red. As Buchanan tells it:

> They found that at the outset the pile looked mostly green, but that, as the pile grew, the green became infiltrated with ever more red. With more grains, the scattering of red danger spots grew until a dense skeleton of instability ran through the pile.

---

[5] Ibid., p. 15.

Here then was a clue to its peculiar behaviour: a grain falling on a red spot can, by domino-like action, cause sliding at nearby red spots. If the red network was sparse, and all trouble spots were well isolated one from the other, then a single grain could have only limited repercussions. But when the red spots came to riddle the pile, the consequences of the next grain become fiendishly unpredictable. It might trigger only a few tumblings, or it might instead set off a cataclysmic chain reaction involving millions.

The sandpile seemed to have configured itself into a hypersensitive and peculiarly unstable condition in which the next falling grain could trigger a response of any size whatsoever.[6]

This unstable condition is what scientists refer to as a "critical state." Scientists had always considered a critical state as a rare occurrence, something that happened infrequently under exceptional circumstances. But the findings from the sandpile game led Bak, Tang and Weisenfeld to ponder a provocative possibility. Again, as Buchanan explains it:

If the critical state arises so easily and inevitably in a simple computer model of a growing sandpile, might something like it also arise elsewhere? Despite what scientists had previously believed, might the critical state in fact be quite common? Could riddling lines of instability of a logically equivalent sort run through the Earth's crust, for example, through forests and ecosystems, and perhaps even through the somewhat more abstract 'fabric' of our economics?[7]

Buried by a Slide

Per Bak's work with his piles of sand and Power Law Distributions caught the attention of other researchers who, in turn, applied it to other areas. Based on their work, it soon became clear that both natural and man-made events — including forest fires, earthquakes, wars and financial crises — followed a Power Law Distribution. When applied to the world of economics, it tells us that we can expect many small financial crises. These will occur with some regularity around the world but their impact will be small and the damage they inflict contained. At the same time, we have to expect the occasional large crisis to engulf us with more cataclysmic results — as it did in 2008.

---

[6]   Buchanan, *Ubiquity*, p. 20.
[7]   Buchanan, *Ubiquity*, p. 21.

The second notable feature of Bak's work that is so crucial to our understanding of financial crises is the knowledge of how an event unfolds. Let's return to our pile of sand. As each new grain of sand lands on the pile, the pile becomes slightly less stable. Each grain of sand within the pile is now, in some degree, unstable. Some grains are relatively stable, yet others are highly unstable and the appearance of even a small external force will cause them to slide.

When several grains of sand in close proximity to one another are unstable, Bak calls this a "finger of instability." As the pile grows, these fingers of instability start to run throughout the sandpile.

Now, imagine that a new grain of sand lands on a vulnerable finger of instability within the sandpile. That will cause the new grain of sand as well as the grains of sand in its immediate vicinity to start sliding. As these grains of sand slide, there is no indication of how big the slide will become. If the initial grains of sand slide into a stable area of the sand pile, the size of the slide will remain small and contained; however, if that slide intersects with more fingers of instability which, in turn, intersect with still more fingers of instability, pretty soon the entire side of the sandpile will give way.

The important concept here: when a landslide begins, its size is not pre-ordained. Instead, the eventual size of the slide depends on the fingers of instability running throughout the sandpile that are encountered by those early-moving grains of sand.[8]

The same appears to be true in financial markets.

Take, for example, the words of Ben Bernanke, then-chairman of the U.S. central bank, the Federal Reserve, during the subprime mortgage crisis that preceded the global credit crunch. He and others repeated the mantra that the problems in subprime mortgages would be contained. "Given the fundamental factors in place that should support the demand for housing, we believe the effect of the troubles in the subprime sector on the broader housing market will likely be limited," he said in a speech to the Federal Reserve Bank of Chicago in May 2007.

Perhaps he was within reason to expect containment, but how wrong he was. The problems in the subprime mortgage market were merely more grains of sand piled onto an economy already riddled with fingers of instability — overheated real estate, overextended consumers and overleveraged financial institutions. One area of instability quickly intersected with other areas of instability until the entire financial sandpile started sliding.

---

[8] Per Bak, *How Nature Works: The Science of Self-Organized Criticality* (New York: Copernicus, 1996).

What began as a problem in one relatively small segment of the market was suddenly a huge landslide engulfing the entire capital market.

From Forests to Finance

There is one more concept to consider: how a financial crisis can seemingly erupt out of nowhere. Hyman Minsky, a Chicago-born, Harvard-educated economist who taught at Washington University in St. Louis, Missouri, put forward the view that long periods of stability often lead to a build-up of instability in a financial system. Since analogies often help us to understand a concept, let's look to the forest for our intuition.

For many years, the forest service in North America tried to protect the forests under their control by immediately suppressing every fire that threatened a productive forest. It certainly seemed like the right thing to do; after all, why allow a fire to destroy a productive forest?

What the forest service had missed was that forest fires are a natural part of the forest ecosystem. In the forest ecosystem, small fires frequently race through the forest, clearing the forest floor of underbrush and allowing new species of plants to lay down roots and thrive. Since the fires were relatively frequent, organic material rarely built up on the forest floor in sufficient quantity to produce a fire of catastrophic proportions.

Once the forest service began protecting the forests, however, these small fires were extinguished before they could perform their natural function. Dead trees and dead brush began to litter the forest floor, creating large amounts of highly flammable fuel. When a fire took hold, as it did in Yellowstone National Park in 1988, it burned hot and was more likely to destroy all of the vegetation in its path. What started as a form of protection had become a danger to the very thing it was trying to protect.

Now, let's return to the financial sector to see how a long period of relative calm can lead, in a somewhat similar fashion, to the build-up of instability.

According to Minsky, when financial markets are calm, investors take on more risk with the hope and expectation of earning a higher rate of return. The longer that period of stability runs, the more confident investors become. As investors' confidence increases, so, too, does their complacency with respect to risk and debt.

When recessions are small and frequent, investors remain vigilant and rarely allow themselves to become overextended. But when many years pass between recessions and investors begin to believe that Big Brother will always be there to protect them from their folly, they inevitably take on more and more debt. Eventually, the risk running through the financial sector overwhelms even the largest Big Brother and a major contraction ensues, just like the forest fire that engulfed Yellowstone.

All this research goes to prove that there is no escaping financial instability. In fact, some instability may be good for us. The economy lets off steam and finds a new equilibrium and investors stay attuned to risk and don't invest foolishly. Bak Per's research coupled with the theories of Hyman Minsky lead us to the conclusion that financial crises will continue to occur. Sometimes they will be small and contained; sometimes they will be large and catastrophic, but we will only know after the fact exactly how each event will end and how far-ranging its effects might be.

What Can You Do to Recover?

- Understand where your fingers of instability are, then take steps to mitigate them.
- Personal debt might be one example of a finger of instability. As long as there are no catastrophic events, the debt is manageable. However, should some triggering event occur, such as job loss, a major health issue or marital breakdown, the fingers of instability in our personal lives begin to intersect.
- The fingers of instability are different for every family unit. Take the time now to understand your own fingers of instability before some landslide overtakes you and your family and buries you.

CHAPTER 9

Interest Rates:
A Primer

ON DECEMBER 16, 2008, the U.S. Federal Reserve dropped the target range for the federal funds rate[1] to 0%-0.25%. Assuming that the Fed maintains this target range for the federal funds rate until mid-2013 as indicated, the United States will have lived with short-term interest rates that are essentially zero for almost five years — an unprecedented event.

Canadian interest rates, although not subject to the same volatility as U.S. rates, have likewise tested new lows. The Canadian target for the overnight rate has been 1% since September 8, 2010. In the ten-year period ended September 2011, the average of the target for the overnight rate was 2.42%, ranging from a high of 4.5% in July 2007 to a low of 0.25% (or twenty-five basis points) in April 2009.

So, what does this mean to the average investor? Are low interest rates good or bad? What causes interest rates to vary and what is the impact of changing interest rates on asset prices?

Interest rates are a topic we cannot escape; they affect our daily lives in many ways. Yet, many investors are fuzzy about what causes rates to vary and what changes might occur when interest rates go up or down. There is good reason for that; the causes — and their effects — are many, and even experts don't always agree on the relationships between the two. But if you

---

[1] The target for the federal funds rate is the rate at which the Federal Reserve would like to see banks lend to each other on an overnight basis. The Canadian equivalent is the target for the overnight rate.

understand how governments use interest rates and monetary policy to attempt to control the economy, you'll have taken another step on the road to financial recovery.

The Cost of Renting

First, what is interest and why do we pay it? The question is not as ridiculous as it might seem, as there is a long history of equating the payment of interest with usury. In the early days of Christianity, the charging of any form of interest was banned. Only Jews were allowed to lend money and charge interest.[2] In more recent years, the term usury has come to represent the charging of interest at an excessive rate.[3]

So what is interest? Interest is simply the price you pay for "renting" money. In much the same way as you would pay to rent an apartment, you also pay to rent or borrow money. Supply and demand of loanable money will influence the rent or interest rate you will pay for that money.

Let's explore the apartment analogy further. When lots of people want to rent apartments but apartments are in short supply, and if the market is allowed to operate freely, rents will rise until supply and demand come into equilibrium. There are two ways that can happen. If builders bring new apartments to market to capture the higher rents, supply will increase to meet demand. Or, if potential renters decide they can't afford an apartment at current prices and withdraw from the market, demand will fall. As supply and demand fluctuates, equilibrium returns to the market. In a similar fashion, interest rates equate the supply and demand for loanable funds.

How are rates determined? When you lend money to someone, you expect compensation from the borrower for the use of your resources. After all, when you lend money, you defer your own ability to consume and expose yourself to several forms of risk, all of which deserve compensation. The compensation you receive for lending money is interest and the amount of interest paid on an investment will be driven by four basic factors:

- the term of the loan,
- the real interest rate when the loan is made,
- our expectations regarding future inflation, and
- our analysis of the riskiness of the borrower.

---

[2] "Usury" found at http://en.wikipedia.org/wiki/Usury, accessed 12 November 2011.

[3] In Canada, the Criminal Code, Section 347, defines the crime of usury as charging an effective annual interest rate that exceeds 60%. Found at http://www.duhaime.org/LegalDictionary/U/Usury.aspx.

In general, the longer the length of time the borrower is renting the money, the greater the risk and, therefore, the more compensation required. The real rate, the expectation for future inflation and the default risk of the borrower are all components of the "nominal" rate, which is the rate that we observe in the market.

In its simplest form, interest rates reflect the price of money.

Of course, nothing is ever that simple. A large number of rates are quoted in the financial press on a wide variety of financial instruments. You will find yields[4] quoted for different maturities of Government of Canada Treasury bills and Treasury bonds, a target for the overnight rate, rates on Banker's Acceptances and guaranteed investment certificates (GICs), the bank rate, the prime rate, mortgage rates and yields on corporate paper, for starters.[5] You do not need to know the intricacies of each of these to appreciate that there are many interest rates that are important.

To complicate things further, there is no one rate that is universally accepted as "the" interest rate for a country, although some are quoted more frequently than others. For example, the prime rate, or the rate commercial banks charge their best borrowing customers, is often quoted. The yield on short-term Treasury bills is another number that is often discussed, as is the Bank of Canada's target for the overnight rate, which is equivalent to the target for the federal funds rate in the U.S.

But this is not as confusing as it might seem, because all interest rates are informally tied together. The yield on short-term Treasury bills, for example, set a floor under all other interest rates or yields in the market. Generally, Treasury bills, which are issued by a country, have no default risk.[6] As well, Treasury bills are issued with maturities of one year or less, with most of the issue volume being near to the short end of the range at three or six months, thereby reducing risk even further.[7] As a result, short-term Treasury bills are often used as a proxy for a risk-free security and their yield as a proxy for the risk-free rate of return. Given their status as

---

[4] In this chapter, we use the terms "rate" and "yield" interchangeably, although it could be argued that there are differences. These differences are not material to our discussion here.

[5] For up-to-date rates, go to Bank of Canada at www.bankofcanada.ca.

[6] This is true in Canada today, but it is not true in all countries. Russia defaulted on its short-term debt in 1998, which shortly thereafter led to the failure of Long-Term Capital Management LP, a U.S.-based hedge fund.

[7] In Canada, Treasury bills are government bonds with a maturity of one year or less. All government bonds with a maturity of more than one year at point of issue are referred to as "Canada bonds" or "long Canadas." In the U.S., the term "Treasury note" refers to government bonds with a maturity of one to ten years.

risk-free securities, it is only natural that the yields on Treasury bills should set a floor under all other rates. When the yield on Treasury bills goes up, all other yields adjust accordingly.

The Nominal Rate

Let's turn our attention to the three basic components of any quoted interest rate. When you observe a quoted interest rate, such as the yield on an AA-rated bond, you will observe what is called the nominal rate. The nominal rate has three separate components: the "real" rate, expected future inflation and a risk premium.

The real rate. The real rate is compensation for deferring consumption. When you lend money, you give up the ability to use that money for the term of the loan. It does not matter whether the money is put on deposit with a bank or used to purchase a bond, the effect is the same — the lender must defer consumption until the loan matures or the bank deposit is withdrawn.

Because the real rate is not directly observable in the market, economists have long debated what the real rate is and what it should be. Until recently, most asserted that the real rate was low and stable. They attributed most of the movement in nominal interest rates to changes in expectations for inflation or changes in issuer risk. However, there is now evidence that real interest rates change substantially over relatively short periods of time. You can see this by looking at bonds that provide a real rate of return to the holder.

Inflation-linked bonds pay a fixed coupon over and above the actual inflation rate as measured by the change in the consumer price index. They have been available in the United Kingdom since 1981, in Canada since 1991 and in the U.S. since 1997.[8] In the United Kingdom, these bonds are called "index-linked gilts." In Canada they are called "real return bonds" and in the U.S., they are known as "TIPS" or "treasury inflation-protected securities."

Let's take the yields on long-term Government of Canada bonds and plot then against the yields on long-term real return bonds using Bank of Canada data from 2001 to 2011. The difference between these two yields is a proxy for investor's expectations for inflation over the period of time until the two bonds mature. In that ten-year period, nominal yields on long Canada bonds trended downward, from about 6% at the start of the period to almost 3% at the end of the period. Yields on real-return bonds also drifted downward, from about 3.7% at the start of the period to about

---

[8]   C. Agathe, Jocelyn Jacob, John Nelmes & Miles Whittingham, "Inflation Expectations and Real Return Bonds," *Bank of Canada Review* (Summer 1996), pp. 41-53.

0.9% at the end of the period. Inflation expectations, on the other hand, remained relatively stable over the ten-year period, moving within a 1% band on either side of the 2% midpoint.

From an investment perspective, which bond is better — the real return bond or the long Canada bond? The answer to this question will be known only once the two bonds have matured, but it will be determined by the course of inflation from today until the maturity date of the bonds. The difference between the real return bond and the long Canada bond in September 2011 is 2.2%. If inflation averages less than 2.2% from that date forward until the maturity date of the bonds, you will be better off investing in the long Canada bond. However, if average inflation is greater than 2.2% over the term of the bonds, you will be better off investing in the real return bond.

Inflation. The expected future inflation rate is a major component of observed nominal interest rates. Wikipedia defines inflation as: "a rise in the general level of prices of goods and services in an economy over a period of time. When the general price level rises, each unit of currency buys fewer goods and services. Consequently, inflation also reflects an erosion in the purchasing power of money — a loss of real value in the internal medium of exchange in the economy. A primary measure of price inflation is the inflation rate, the annualized percentage change in a general price index (normally the consumer price index) over time."[9]

In simple terms, inflation erodes the purchasing power of money. More money is required to purchase the same basket of goods and services. Because a lender wants to earn a positive rate of return on his or her money, the lender needs to be compensated for both the deferral of his or her own consumption, as well as any loss of purchasing power the principal might suffer as a result of inflation. If lenders don't obtain sufficient compensation for inflation, as often happens during periods of rising inflation, the real return earned on their money is negative. For example, from 1966 to 1981, bond investors in the U.S. had a negative real annual compound rate of return of 4.2%,[10] meaning the real value of their bond investment declined at the rate of 4.2% a year. During that period of high and rising inflation, bond investors consistently underestimated the impact of inflation on their securities.

Risk premium. The third component of the nominal rate is a risk premium. If a short-term Treasury bill is a risk-free security and the rate on

---

[9] "Inlation," *Wikipedia*, found at: http://en.wikipedia.org/wiki/Inflation, accessed 12 November 2011.

[10] Professor Jeremy Siegel, found at http://www.jeremysiegel.com.

that short-term Treasury bill represents a risk-free rate of return, then all other rates can be quoted as some premium over and above the risk-free rate. What kinds of risk are captured in a risk premium? Although there are several, the most important risks are default risk, interest-rate risk and reinvestment risk.

Default risk takes into account the possibility that the borrower will not repay the borrowed funds according to the contract. The borrower may either refuse to pay or be unable to pay, but the effect on the lender is the same. Should a borrower not pay interest in the amount required at the time it is due, the lender will not earn the expected rate of return on the loan. To compensate for this possibility, the lender will attempt to classify borrowers according to their default risk. As default risk rises, so does the interest rate charged.

Interest-rate risk refers to the change in the price of a bond due to a change in market yields. The longer the bond's maturity and the lower the bond's coupon, the greater is the interest-rate risk. In an environment of falling interest rates, the lender is happy to lend long term as bond prices rise when interest rates fall. However, if interest rates are rising, the lender wants to lend short term to protect against capital losses.

Reinvestment risk occurs when periodic interest payments have to be reinvested at market rates that differ from the yield to maturity on the original investment. For example, assume that you hold a ten year bond with a 5% yield to maturity when purchased. If interest rates drop significantly, each coupon will have to be reinvested at a rate significantly below the original 5% yield to maturity. The higher the bond's coupon, the greater the reinvestment risk, as there is more cash flow to be reinvested.

Interest Rates and Monetary Policy

So, you have an understanding of the basics of interest rates. But what do interest rates have to do with monetary policy?

Governments have two basic policies they use to influence their economies: fiscal policy and monetary policy. Fiscal policy involves decisions around taxation and spending; monetary policy involves the use of interest rates to affect economic behaviour.

When a central bank wants to cool down an overheating economy, it "pulls on the interest rate string." In other words, it forces interest rates higher. As the cost of borrowing becomes more expensive, people borrow less, causing consumption and investment expenditures to fall. Eventually, the economy slows under the weight of the higher rates.

Alternately, when a central bank wants to stimulate an economy, it "pushes on the interest rate string." In other words, it lowers interest rates, making borrowing cheaper. Normally, that induces people to borrow and spend more, which in turn drives economic growth.

There are two issues that arise out of this. First, what interest rate can the central bank directly influence? Second, why does monetary policy appear to be impotent in today's world? Let's start with the first question.

In both Canada and the U.S., the central banks directly influence the overnight rate. In Canada, the Bank of Canada publishes a target for the overnight rate, which is set at the mid-point of the operating band. The operating band is a fifty-basis-point spread centered on the target for the overnight rate. So, if the target for the overnight rate is 1%, the Bank of Canada will ensure that overnight interest rates in Canada will remain between 0.75% and 1.25%. The Bank of Canada has several tools it can use to maintain the overnight interest rate within the operating band, but the two primary ones are known as "repos" and "reverse repos."

Suppose the Bank of Canada observes that overnight interest rates are threatening to breach the lower end of the operating band of 0.75% because there is an excess of liquidity in the banking system. It will enter the market and offer to sell Treasury bills on an overnight basis to any financial institution with excess liquidity, buying them back the next day at a slightly higher price. The sale and repurchase prices are set such that the annualized interest rate is exactly equal to the lower end of the operating band. Of course, no profit-maximizing bank would place money overnight at a rate less than what it could get from the Bank of Canada.

A similar thing happens if the Bank of Canada believes that a shortage of liquidity will drive the overnight rate above the upper end of the operating band. In that case, the Bank of Canada will offer to buy Treasury bills from any financial institution that needs cash, selling them back to the bank the next day at a slightly higher price, with the price differential again equating to an annualized interest rate equal to the upper end of the operating band.

Now that you understand some basic factors about monetary policy, you might ask why interest rates have been stuck at essentially zero for such a long time. Do we run the risk of becoming another Japan, where interest rates have been close to zero for almost twenty years?

The answer to this question goes right to the heart of our present crisis. Normally, when a central bank drops interest rates, the lower rates induce both companies and consumers to borrow and spend more money. This has been working beautifully in Canada, with consumers gleefully ramping up their personal indebtedness as they snap up the latest bargains. But in the U.S., both companies and consumers have become much less inclined to assume more debt. With house prices continuing to fall and "true" unemployment and underemployment running at close to 20%, consumers are focused on repairing their personal balance sheets. They are trying to pay down debt and save for retirement. Because consumers don't want to spend, companies are loath to invest. Thus, even with rates at multi-decade lows, U.S. borrowers are not rushing to take advantage of the easy credit that is available.

What will persuade the U.S. borrower to take on new debt? The one word answer is "confidence." Only when confidence in the future returns will that American once again begin to borrow and spend.

What Can You Do to Recover?

- Interest rates are the price you pay to borrow or rent money.
- Central banks have signalled that short-term policy rates are not expected to rise, in Canada not until 2012 and in the U.S., not until 2013.
- When interest rates are low but expected to rise, protect yourself against capital losses by lending short term with a high coupon.
- In a falling interest-rate environment, try to lend long term with a low coupon to maximize yield.
- The only bond with no reinvestment risk is the "zero coupon bond," as there is no intermediate cash flow to be reinvested.
- The bond with the maximum interest rate risk is the zero coupon bond, as it has all of its cash flow occurring on the maturity date.

CHAPTER 10

Inflation: Just Another Form of Taxation

YOU MAY BE WARY OF INFLATION because you know that inflation makes the goods and services you buy more expensive, seriously eroding your purchasing power and your future wealth. But inflation has a role to play in reducing public sector debt. And given that governments have only four mechanisms for dealing with too much debt — increased taxation, reduced government spending, default or inflation — there is a significant probability that inflation will once again rear its ugly head in at least some Western nations.

There is good reason to fear inflation's impact on your financial well-being. In an inflationary economy, one unit of the domestic currency will purchase fewer goods and services over time. In a severely inflationary environment, usually referred to as "hyperinflation," the value of the currency, as measured by the goods and services it can purchase, can fall on a daily basis. It can soon wipe out your ability to buy the good and services you need.

Consider the bond investor who wants to realize a yield that compensates him or her for both the deferral of consumption (the real interest rate) and the loss of future purchasing power that occurs due to inflation. When inflation is stable, the compensation for the loss of purchasing power is built into the nominal rate. The problem arises when inflation unexpectedly spikes upward after a bond or other fixed-income instrument has been purchased. In this case, the yield-to-maturity that the bond was purchased to provide is not sufficient to compensate for the unexpected loss of purchasing power.

Let's take a simple example. Assume that you purchase a $1,000 government bond that matures in ten years and that, at the time you bought it, that $1,000 would purchase a bundle of goods and services equivalent in value. Ten years later, good to its word, the government returns the $1,000 face value of the bond. But, in the meantime, inflation has made a comeback in year ten and it is now 5%. Because of inflation, the goods and services that you can purchase with that $1,000 has shrunk to $1,000 less 5% or $950.

That is in one year. Over a long period of time, even relatively small amounts of inflation can be highly destructive to wealth. Let's consider another example. Suppose you believe that inflation is going to average 2% a year for the next ten years, which is about what we expect Canada's inflation to be. Based on this, you buy a ten-year Government of Canada bond carrying a 3% yield-to-maturity, based on your assumption that the 3% nominal rate will provide approximately a 1% real rate of return and 2% to offset expected future inflation.[1]

However, instead of averaging 2%, inflation averages 5% over the ten-year period. With 2% inflation, something that costs $100 today will cost $122 in ten years. However, if inflation increases to five percent, the good that costs $100 today will cost $163 in ten years. Note that in this example, inflation goes up from 2% to 5%, an increase of 150%, but the cost of today's $100 bundle of goods and services rises from $122 (with 2% inflation) to $163 (with 5% inflation), an increase of 186% in the inflation adjustment.

Thanks to compounding, the percentage increase in cost is much greater than the percentage increase in inflation.

Inflation as a Form of Taxation

Inflation is sometimes described as just another form of taxation, although the reason for that may not be clear from the foregoing. To understand why inflation is just another form of taxation, let's work through another example.

First, any form of taxation is simply a transfer of purchasing power from Party A to Party B. With an income tax, the taxpayer transfers purchasing power to the taxing authority by physically transferring cash or bank balances from the taxpayer's account to the taxing authority's bank account. With the inflation tax, the transfer of purchasing power is

---

[1] The exact formulation of the Fisher Equation includes the cross product term (the interaction between the real rate and the inflation rate). However, the approximation to the Fisher Equation, which can be stated as: Nominal Rate = Real Rate + Expected Future Inflation, is relatively accurate when expected inflation is low.

less obvious but equally real. This time the transfer of purchasing power is from creditors to debtors. In Canada and the U.S., as in most countries, the largest debtor is the federal government.

The transfer of purchasing power works like this: the government issues a fixed-coupon, long-term bond. Let's assume that the bond in question has a $1,000 face value, a 3% coupon and ten years to maturity. The bond sells in the market at par, based on an inflation expectation of 2% and a real return expectation of about 1%. After the bond is issued, the central bank allows several years of 5% inflation. At the bond's maturity date, the government returns the $1,000 to the holder of the bond plus the final coupon. But, because of inflation, the $1,000 face value will now purchase only $632 worth of goods and services. The bond's issuer has effectively confiscated $368 of the bond investor's wealth. A portion of this $368 confiscation of wealth was anticipated and is compensated for by the 2% portion of the coupon that is allocated to inflation. However, the larger portion of the $368 was unanticipated and this is the inflation tax.

There has been an effective transfer of wealth from the bond investor to the bond's issuer. Although the bond's coupon of 3% compensated for a portion of the loss in purchasing power, it is not sufficient to offset the loss of purchasing power resulting from unexpected inflation.

Inflation has produced a confiscation of wealth that is every bit as real as the impact of income taxes, but it is so insidious that most investors are never aware that a portion of their wealth has been expropriated.

It is for this reason that heavily indebted, weak governments have always used inflation as a policy tool. As long as a government's debt is held by the domestic population and denominated in the domestic currency, a government can inflate its way back to fiscal solvency. The holders of long-term government bonds become the willing — and, often, unwitting — taxpayers who make it possible.

Had Greece retained its own currency, the drachma, and had it issued bonds denominated only in drachmas, there would be no talk about a Greek default. Instead, Greece would have monetized its government debt[2] by selling government bonds to its central bank until the desired amount

---

[2] A central bank "monetizes" government debt by exchanging a liability that is not money (a Treasury bill) for a liability that is money (currency). Note that paper currency is simply a liability of the central bank. The offsetting asset for most central banks is Treasury bills and Treasury bonds issued by the government.

of inflation had occurred and the country was able to function normally again. As the central bank printed more drachmas in exchange for the government debt it was buying, the value of the drachma would fall in the foreign-exchange market, making Greek exports cheaper for foreign buyers and imports into Greece more expensive for Greek consumers. Eventually, this adjustment mechanism would return the country's economy to good health, without having to lower its citizen's nominal incomes. The same holds true for Italy and the lira.

A government that can print its own currency and that issues debt denominated only in its own currency will never default. It will simply redeem its debt with a depreciated currency that will purchase fewer goods and services than it formerly did.

For a similar reason, the U.S. government will default on its debt only if it is not allowed to issue more debt or if the Fed refuses to purchase debt issued by the government. As long as the government has the ability to create new debt and as long as the Fed is willing to monetize the debt of the government, the U.S. government will never default on its debt — although the holders of that debt may suffer significant losses in wealth.

This does not mean that the purchase of long-term government bonds is a bad idea. It just means that a bond investor must remain vigilant to the changes in inflation that might erode the purchasing power or the real value of the bond's face value.

The Distorting Effects of Inflation

As if the expropriation of wealth caused by unexpected inflation is not enough, inflation also causes major distortions because the *nominal* amount of interest received is taxed, not the *real* amount. Have you ever heard anybody say: "Oh, but for the good old days when I used to be able to live on the interest income from my investments?"

Consider the following scenario: a retiree is living on the income from a large portfolio, which is invested entirely in fixed-income securities. The senior's income tax rate is 25%. Based on these assumptions, let's construct the following table, showing the real, after-tax return earned on the portfolio. For simplicity, we will assume four inflation scenarios: 0%, 5%, 10% and 15%, each of which is associated with a 5% real interest rate.

The real after-tax return on a fixed-income portfolio

A	B	C	D	E
			After-tax	After-tax
		Nominal rate	nominal rate*	real rate**
Inflation rate	Real rate	C=A+B	D=C(1-T)	E=D-A
(%)	(%)	(%)	(%)	(%)
0.0	5.0	5.0	3.75	3.75
5.0	5.0	10.0	7.5	2.5
10.0	5.0	15.0	11.25	1.25
15.0	5.0	20.0	15.0	0.0

* The after-tax amount is calculated as: After-tax = (Pre-tax)(1 − tax rate). Thus, with 0% inflation, the nominal after-tax rate is calculated as: (5%)(1 − 0.25%) = 3.75%.
** The after-tax real return is computed by subtracting the inflation rate from the after-tax nominal return.

Source: Robert Ironside

The retiree living in a 0%-inflation world earns the highest after-tax real rate of return (as shown in Column E). The retiree living in the highest nominal interest-rate environment earns the lowest after-tax rate of return. In the early 1980s, when inflation and interest rates spiraled into the double digits, the retirees who thought they were living off their interest income were suffering from what economists call "money illusion," which occurs when investors are oblivious to the actual impact of inflation and taxes.

Although it is immediately obvious that the person living in a world with 20% nominal interest rates is receiving a large annual interest income, it is a little more difficult to decipher the effects of inflation on income. What is not so obvious is that the purchasing power of the portfolio is declining by the rate of inflation or 15% a year, making the after-tax real return zero. The effect of the decrease in residual purchasing power in the high-inflation environment is exactly the same as consuming a portion of the principal every year in a zero-inflation environment. The only difference between the person in the low-inflation environment and the person in the high-inflation environment is the person in the low-inflation environment is painfully aware of how much capital he or she is consuming. The person in the high-inflation environment is often blissfully unaware of how much his or her capital is being eroded.

The higher the personal tax bracket, of course, the more pronounced is the distortion thanks to the taxation of nominal interest rates, not real rates. Let's take our retiree with his large portfolio of fixed-income securities and up his average personal tax rate to 50%. We see something that looks like this:

The impact of income taxes on real returns

A	B	C	D	E
Inflation rate (%)	Real rate (%)	Nominal rate C=A+B (%)	Nominal After-tax rate* D=C(1-T) (%)	Real After-tax rate of return** E=D-A (%)
0.0	5.0	5.0	2.5	2.5
5.0	5.0	10.0	5.0	0.0
10.0	5.0	15.0	7.5	-2.5
15.0	5.0	20.0	10.0	-5.0

* The after-tax amount is always calculated as (Pre-tax)(1 – tax rate). Thus, for 0% inflation, the nominal after-tax rate is calculated as: (5%)(1 – 0.25) = 3.75%

** The after-tax amount is always calculated as (Pre-tax)(1 – tax rate). Thus, for 0% inflation, the nominal after-tax rate is calculated as: (5%)(1 - .25) = 3.75%

Source: Robert Ironside

In the above table, the impact of high tax rates coupled with high inflation becomes even more destructive, as the after-tax real return becomes negative in the high-inflation world. This is a scenario that many investors will probably face at some future date, as the world's governments deleverage.

The important take-away is that you must focus on after-tax real returns, not pre-tax nominal returns.

To get another perspective on the wealth-destroying ability of inflation, you have only to look at the inflation calculator on the Bank of Canada website.[3] This is a great tool for quickly and simply calculating the effect of inflation between any two years from 1914 to the present. For example, a basket of goods and services that cost $100 in 1914 would require $2,044.07 to purchase in the summer of 2011. The total percentage increase in the cost of living since 1914 is 1,944%.

This works out to an average annual inflation rate of 3.16% over the ninety-seven-year period. In a world in which people are retiring earlier and living longer, the probability of out-living our savings becomes a very distinct possibility. Should a future government allow spending and inflation to take hold again, as it did in the 1970s, this is a problem that everybody will face, no matter how fiscally prudent they have been.

---

[3] Inflation calculator, Bank of Canada, found at: http://www.bankofcanada.ca/rates/related/inflation-calculator/, accessed 13 November 2011.

In the End

Inflation is an erosion of purchasing power caused by the supply of money rising faster than the supply of goods and services that can be purchased with that money. In its most extreme form, usually referred to as hyperinflation, the effects can be devastating and far-reaching.

Even relatively small amounts of inflation over long periods of time can lead to a significant increase in the cost of what you buy. This is of most concern to people on pensions and fixed incomes that are not indexed to the cost of living. It is also of great concern to the investor purchasing fixed-income securities

What Can You Do to Recover?

- Inflation is likely to return in at least some countries, although when this might happen is impossible to tell.
- To prevent large capital losses, keep bond durations relatively short.
- Remember that preferred shares are a form of fixed-income security and will go down in price if inflation rises.
- Do be careful about chasing yield by lengthening the maturity of the bond portfolio. A small increase in yield today can be quickly eliminated by large capital losses in the future.
- Inflation is another form of tax. It erodes wealth. Certain tax provisions are not indexed to inflation; for example unused RRSP contribution room. To build more real wealth, contribute sooner, rather than later, to your RRSP.

CHAPTER 11

Asset Prices: A Time and Money Machine

WITHOUT DOUBT, inflation and interest rates have an impact on the value of your financial assets now and in the future. But there is little you, as an individual, can do to control the economic storms they can unleash. Monetary and fiscal policies are the domain of government.

But there are steps you can take to control the risk interest rates and inflation present to your investment portfolio. It requires understanding the influences that affect the value of your assets, researching diligently your investment opportunities and choosing carefully the securities that go into your portfolio.

The Market Price

In general, the market price of any asset is equal to the present value of the future income stream that it generates. This insight allows us to calculate an intrinsic or "fair value" price for any asset, as long as we can determine:
- the amount of the asset's cash flows,
- the timing of the asset's cash flows, and
- the discount rate to apply to those cash flows based on expectations of future events.

The model works well for any asset that generates a cash-flow stream over time. It falls apart, for example, when we try to value gold, which has no periodic cash-flow stream. It does, however, work very well for bonds and almost as well for equities.

Bond Prices and Interest Rates

Bonds generate two streams of cash flow:

- the periodic coupon, or the rate at which interest is paid on the bond, and
- the face value at maturity.

As both the amount of the coupon and the face value are typically fixed and the timing of payment is predetermined, the only variable is the discount rate that is applied to bond's cash flows.

So, the first basic rule to remember: the discount rate rises as the present value of the income stream goes down, and vice versa. Therefore, bonds go up in price when interest rates fall and they fall in price when interest rates go up. Second, the further away in time the cash flow occurs, the greater the impact of changing the discount rate. That means long bonds have much greater price volatility than short bonds and low-coupon bonds have greater price volatility than high-coupon bonds.[1] The most volatile of all are zero-coupon bonds with long maturities.

How do these rules apply in today's environment? It suggests that Operation Twist — launched by U.S. Federal Reserve on September 21, 2011 — created significant risk for the buyers of long bonds. Operation Twist was designed to flatten the "yield curve," which is a closely watched indicator of interest rate movements. The yield curve takes bonds of equal quality but differing maturity and plots the yields against the maturities; a "normal" yield curve slopes upward as longer-term bonds have higher rates because of the risk attached to longer maturities. Operation Twist's goal was to "twist" yields at the long end of the curve downward, forcing long-term rates lower. To accomplish this objective, the Fed started selling the short-term government bonds it had accumulated as a result of its quantitative easing programs and buying long-term Treasury bonds. By the time the programs ends in summer 2012, the fed will have increased the demand for long Treasuries by roughly $400 billion. This extra demand should push up the price of long bonds, which in turn will cause yields to fall, pushing long-term interest rates lower. Mortgages, car loans, loans to buy plants and machinery become a lot more attractively priced.

There is little doubt that the Fed was on the right track: the mere antic-ipation of Operation Twist pushed rates on ten-year Treasury bonds to

---

[1] A greater proportion of a low-coupon bond's total cash flows occurs on the maturity date than a high-coupon bond's. Thus, a low-coupon bond has an effective maturity date that is further away in time than an otherwise identical bond with a higher coupon. This concept is captured in the calculation of the bond's duration, a topic that is not dealt with in this text.

around 1.8% and yields on 30-year Treasury bonds to less than 3%.[2] But what happens come summer 2012, when the program ends? Will long rates remain low?

And that is the danger for bond investors today. If Operation Twist has the desired effect and stimulates demand, the increased confidence in the economy that ensues will cause upward pressure on long rates.

Unless the buyers of long-dated securities are extremely careful, they will incur large capital losses as long bond prices fall and yields rise toward more normal levels.

There are other reasons unwary investors should be cautious about bonds when interest rates are volatile. Many bonds are sold with a "call" feature that allows the issuer to repurchase the bond under specific conditions. From the issuer's perspective, exercising the call makes most sense when interest rates have fallen sufficiently low that it is economical to call the existing issue and refinance with a new issue. This is not so great for the bondholder, who is forced to sell a bond with a high yield and replace it with one that has a low yield. Call features can present significant risk for the uninitiated.

On the other hand, another bond feature, a "put option," can mitigate interest-rate risk. A put option allows the bondholder the option to "put" or sell the bond back to the issuer at a fixed price over a fixed period of time. The put option will be most useful to the bondholder during a period of rising interest rates, as bond prices fall as yields rise. By exercising the put option, the bondholder is able to recoup most or all of his or her investment, which can then be reinvested at the higher yields available in the marketplace.

Likewise, "convertible" bonds provide another avenue of protection for bond investors. A convertible bond is normally convertible into a fixed number of common shares at either a fixed conversion price or a fixed conversion ratio. If economic activity is strong, share prices are generally expected to rise. On the other hand, strong economic activity could push interest rates higher — and bond prices lower. If bond prices are falling, the conversion feature may be valuable. By converting the bond into common shares, the bondholder can potentially mitigate the negative impact of higher interest rates (and falling bond prices which that

---

[2] "Daily Treasury Yield Curve Rates," U.S. Department of the Treasury, found at: http://www.treasury.gov/resource-center/data-chart-center/interest-rates/Pages/TextView.aspx?data=yield, accessed 15 November 2011.

implies) by converting into an instrument that will rise in value with the economic upturn.

Bonds are not for the faint of heart but they can offer some excellent investment opportunities at the right time during the economic cycle.

Stock Prices and Interest Rates

If the price of any financial asset is simply the present value of the expected future cash flows generated by the asset, how does that apply to equities or stocks? After all, for bonds, calculating the cash flows is fairly straightforward: the interest payments in the form of the coupon and the face value received at maturity are established when the bond is issued. Certainly, you can calculate the expected future cash flows a stock generates — the dividend — but, unlike a bond, a stock has no maturity or expiry date. When issued, a common stock is assumed to last until infinity. Therefore, the concept of a maturity value does not hold.

But even dividends do not produce a completely reliable income stream. Dividend rates on typical preferred shares are fixed but dividends on common shares are not. Some publicly traded companies never pay dividends, others are very consistent payers of dividends.

So, when calculating the market price for a common stock, we make certain assumptions. We assume dividends will grow at a relatively constant rate. Given the lack of a maturity date, we assume the stock will last to infinity and thus value it as a perpetuity based on its dividend stream. The discount rate applied to the dividend stream is determined by the riskiness of the expected future dividend stream, with a higher risk implying a higher discount rate and thus a lower price.

If we apply this model in today's low interest rate environment, we might expect the low discount rate to push stock prices higher. However, the reason for the low interest rates — a massive economic downturn in the global economy — could be seen as pushing risk higher. The net effect of these opposing forces is difficult to calculate, as perceptions of risk vary from day to day, leading to large price swings in the major stock indices around the world. This volatility will probably remain until there is some resolution to the sovereign debt problems in Europe, Japan and the United States.

Forecasting the Future of Interest Rates

Given that the prices of both stocks and bonds are so intimately connected to interest rates, what would be truly helpful is if we could forecast future interest rates. That would go a long way to helping us determine future stock and bond prices. Unfortunately, that is no easy task. Interest rates are affected by the policy actions of central banks as well as the actions of investors and savers around the globe. What we can do, however, is look to the yield curve and see what its shape can tell us about the future direction of interest rates.

First, remember that the yield curve, or "term structure," is simply a plot of the yields of a certain quality of bond across a wide range of maturities. Government securities are normally used, as governments are the only issuers with enough breadth and depth of coverage to have bonds that span the whole the maturity spectrum.

The "unbiased expectations theory of the term structure" posits that the long-term interest rate is the geometric average of intervening short-term rates. An upward sloping term structure would suggest that future short rates are expected to be higher than current short rates. Conversely, a downward sloping term structure would suggest that future short rates are expected to be lower than current short rates.

Given how tightly interest rates and economic activity are linked, it would make intuitive sense that an upward sloping term structure is also indicative of rising economic activity and a downward or "inverted" term structure is indicative of falling economic activity. This intuition is borne out by research done by the Bank of Canada. In an article entitled, "The Term Structure of Interest Rates as a Leading Economic Indicator: A Technical Note,"[3] the author notes that:

> The spread between long-term and short-term interest rates has proven to be an excellent predictor of changes of economic activity in Canada. As a general rule, when long-term interest rates have been much above short-term rates, strong increases in output have followed within about a year; however, whenever the yield curve has been inverted for any extended period of time, a recession has followed. Similar findings exist for other countries, including the United States. Although Canadian and U.S. interest rates generally move quite closely together, the Canadian yield curve has been distinctly better at predicting future Canadian output. The explanation given for this result is that the term spread has reflected both current monetary conditions, which affect short-term interest rates, and expected real returns on investment and expectations of inflation, which are the main determinants of long-term rates.

---

[3] Kevin Clinton, "The Term Structure of Interest Rates as a Leading Economic Indicator: A Technical Note," *Bank of Canada Review,* Winter 1994-1995.

In Summary

Let's not forget that the market price of any asset is the present value of the expected future cash flows generated by the asset. Bonds generate two future cash flows: the coupon payment and the face value at maturity. The longer the maturity of the bond and the lower the coupon, the more volatile the bond's price will be. Short-term bonds with high coupons have less price volatility than long bonds with low coupons. Call options, put options and conversion features can either increase or decrease the risk of a bond investment.

Intrinsic stock prices are often calculated as the present value of the stock's expected future cash flow. As interest rates fall, stock prices should rise and vice versa. However, since interest rates are often driven by economic activity, a falling interest rate is often associated with weakening economic activity, which in turn might indicate falling stock prices.

What Can You Do to Recover?

- Low interest rates are good for borrowers but they are not good for retirees living off of the earnings from their investments.
- Low, short-term interest rates will probably be here until at least 2013.
- Operation Twist has been driving U.S. long-term rates downward and will continue to do so until the summer of 2012. If Operation Twist is successful, economic growth will resume in late 2012, investor confidence will increase and long rates will be forced higher. This will lead to capital losses for those investors who didn't sell their long bonds before long rates started to rise.
- Rising long rates will confer capital losses on the holders of long bonds.
- Rising long rates may or may not drive down stock prices. The impact on stock prices will depend on the relative weight given to a rising discount rate versus stronger future economic activity leading to higher dividends.

CHAPTER 12

Volatility: The New Normal?

WHO CAN BLAME YOU for refusing to open your brokerage statement, knowing the bad news it contains. The years since 2000 have not been easy ones for investors, and the 2008 meltdown has only intensified our despair.

So what happened? How could markets go from so good — a nineteen-year bull market — to so volatile? Why do markets appear to race higher one day, only to fall precipitously the next? More to the point, when can we expect a return to the good old days, before 2000, when share prices moved upward uninterrupted?

It's time to get your expectations in line: that is not likely to happen any time soon. By all accounts, the market volatility that has marked recent years isn't going anywhere. In fact, many believe volatility is the "new normal."

The New Normal

According to Jeremy Siegel, the highly regarded Wharton finance professor and author,[1] the period from 1981 to 1999 was the greatest bull market in U.S. history. During that period, the U.S. stock market returned a real, average annual compound return of 13.6%.[2]

---

[1] Jeremy Siegel, Stocks for the Long Run (New York, McGraw Hill, 1994) and *The Future for Investors: Why the Tried and the True Triumph Over the Bold and the New* (New York: Crown Business, 2005).

[2] www.jeremysiegel.com

What would that mean if you had invested in the stock market during this period? Let's say that you invested $10,000 in the Standard & Poor's 500 composite index, a proxy for the U.S. stock market, on January 1, 1981. By December 31, 1999, nineteen years later, that $10,000 investment had a nominal value of $206,000.[3] Of course, inflation would have eaten away some of its purchasing power, but the real purchasing power of the $10,000 investment was still $105,600.

It is easy to get spoiled with returns like those. You come to expect that somehow, this is the norm, and you are entitled to double-digit annual returns over long periods of time.

Unfortunately, the first decade of the 2000s has not been kind to investors. Had you invested another $10,000 in the S&P 500 on January 1, 2000, by December 31, 2010, the investment would have been worth a nominal $10,400, after growing at an average annual compound rate of 0.31%. Subtract the loss of purchasing power because of inflation and the real purchasing power of our $10,000 investment falls to $7,900.

Why was the period from 1981 to 1999 so positive for stocks and why has the last decade been so abysmal? Are invisible forces driving the market? Or is there a credible reason for the stomach-churning volatility of the recent past?

First, let's define what is meant by volatility. Volatility, from a technical perspective, refers to the "standard deviation" of a security's return. Very simply, standard deviation is a quantitative measure of how tightly returns are clustered around the average return. A simple example will make this definition more concrete. We have two stocks, A and B. Both stocks have an average monthly return of 1%, but the monthly returns of Stock A range from -10% to +10%. The monthly returns for Stock B, on the other hand, range from -2% to +2%. Stock A has a much higher standard deviation, since the range of actual returns is much wider.

So how volatile is the market? To get an anecdotal sense of market volatility, we turn to a report from Reuters online news service: "Over the summer [2011], the S&P 500 index, a broad measure of U.S. large-cap stocks, crashed 17% in just fourteen trading days between July 21 and August 10. For investors, that was one of the most trying periods on record, and they are just not ready to start taking on big bets."[4]

---

[3] Moneychimp, found at: http://www.moneychimp.com/features/market_cagr.htm, accessed 14 November 2011.

[4] Edward Krudy, "Volatility stymies even smart money," Reuters, 16 September 2011, found at: http://finance.yahoo.com/news/Analysis-Volatility-stymies-rb-1372874464.html?x=0&. v=1, accessed 16 September 2011.

A more quantitative measure of volatility is the Chicago Board Options Exchange Market Volatility Index, or VIX, a popular measure of the implied volatility of the S&P 500. Often referred to as the "fear index" or the "fear gauge,"[5] it is a measure of the market's expectation of stock market volatility over the next thirty days. "The VIX is quoted in percentage points and translates, roughly, to the expected movement in the S&P 500 index over the next thirty-day period, which is then annualized."[6]

In October 2008, the VIX spiked sharply as the world teetered on the edge of the financial abyss, signaling the yo-yoing markets that followed. It then dropped significantly, before rising again in the late summer of 2011, driven by fears of a U.S. recession and a sovereign debt default in Europe. We know what happened next.

So, what is the cause of these wild price fluctuations? As with most things to do with markets, there is never just one answer. If it were really that easy, every investor would be rich and living his or her dream. Reality is rarely that kind and understanding the markets is always difficult.

Price/Earnings Ratio

Let's first look at price/earnings ratio (P/E), a good indicator of investor sentiment. While not a cause of market volatility, the P/E gives us a quantitative measure of the "mood" of the market.

To calculate the P/E ratio, you divide a publicly traded company's current price per share by its earnings per share for the most recent four quarters. The resulting number tells us what investors are willing to pay for each $1 of corporate earnings. When investors are confident and feel that the future is bright, they are willing to pay more and the P/E ratios rise. When investors are more bearish about the future, P/E ratios fall.

For example, in August 1982, the average P/E for the five hundred large-cap, American stocks that make up the S&P 500 was less than 7, indicating investors were willing to pay around $7 a share for $1 of earnings. Then, the average P/E exploded upward for the next eighteen years, peaking at 44 in the year 2000. P/E values then fell precipitously, reaching an average of 12 in the spring of 2009.

What does this change in the average P/E imply for the share price of a stock traded on the U.S. market? Suppose you bought ABC Corporation in August 1982, when its earnings per share were $1 and the average P/E of the S&P 500 was 7. You paid $7 a share for ABC. Now, let's assume that ABC continues to earn $1 a share for the next eighteen years and the market

---

5   "VIX" Wikipedia, found at http://en.wikipedia.org/wiki/VIX, accessed 16 September 2011.
6   Ibid.

continues to price ABC stock at the average P/E for the market. What is ABC stock worth in the year 2000? Using a market average P/E of 44, ABC is now worth $44 a share.

ABC's share price rose by almost 11% a year, even though the company's earnings were exactly the same as they were in 1982. You could be forgiven for thinking that the share price escalated in value because of your superior intellect and foresight in choosing such a wonderful stock. Why else would its share price climb to $44 a share from $7 a share? But you would be wrong. Just as you would be wrong for thinking you were an idiot and ABC was a dog in the period that followed. Even though ABC continued to pump out earnings per share of $1 every year for the next nine years, its share price sank. ABC stock opened the decade at $44 a share and ended 2009 at $12 a share.

The reality is the share price of ABC rose from $7 a share in 1982 to $44 a share in 2000 and then fell to $12 a share in 2009 because of changing investor sentiment. You and many other investors were simply victims of market moods. This speaks to a basic truth about investing: if you enter the market when values (as measured by P/Es) are high, you will probably do poorly and earn a relatively low rate of return. If, on the other hand, you enter the market when values are low and ride the upward cycle, you will do well.

But, more to the point, what made investor sentiment change? Let's look at the economic events of the time. In the early 1980s, North America was just coming out of a deep, double-dip recession induced by the U.S. Federal Reserve's bid to squeeze inflation out of the U.S. economy. By then, the inflation dragon that had ruled the 1970s had been slain, and president Ronald Reagan's tax cuts were propelling the market forward. Markets got another boost in the 1990s when the information technology revolution took hold and investors were happy to believe that this time was different, earnings weren't important and stock prices would go up forever.

Unfortunately, they, too, got their comeuppance. The "tech bubble" burst in March 2000; the NASDAQ-100 index, which includes one hundred of the largest domestic and international non-financial securities listed on the Nasdaq Stock Market,[7] fell back to earth, bringing investor sentiment and P/E ratios with it.[8] The U.S. economy contracted soon thereafter. Investor confidence had been shaken and negative sentiment had arrived.

---

[7]   More information on the NASDAQ-100 index and the Nasdaq Stock Market can be found at: http://www.nasdaq.com/markets/indices/nasdaq-100.aspx, accessed 16 November 2011.

[8]   From its market peak of 5,048 on March 10, 2000, the NASDAQ-100 index fell to 1,139 on October 4, 2002, a loss of 77% in market value in two and a half years.

So, what does this tell us about the factors that drive market performance? *P/E ratios are an indicator of market sentiment, not a cause of market behaviour.*

Efficient Markets or Irrational Investors?

Forty years ago, Eugene Fama, a finance professor at the Booth School of Business at University of Chicago, popularized the concept known as the "efficient market hypothesis" or EMH. The EMH postulates that stock prices are "informationally efficient" which means that prices are driven strictly by the flow of information and the current stock price is always the "correct" price. When new information is received, the stock price will respond quickly to its receipt, either rising or falling as the new information is factored into the price. Because new information is received in random and unpredictable WAYS, stock prices must also move in random and unpredictable ways.[9]

Fama went on to suggest there were three forms of informational efficiency:

- weak-form efficiency,
- semi-strong form efficiency, and
- strong-form efficiency.

If a market is weak-form efficient, then all information contained in the past record of stock prices and trading volumes is already captured in the current stock price. In a weak-form efficient market, it is impossible to earn excess profits consistently through the use of technical analysis, which employs charts depicting past stock-price and volume information.

If a market is semi-strong form efficient, the current stock price captures all information currently in the public domain. Finally, if a market is strong-form efficient, the current stock price captures all information in both the public and the private domains.[10] In other words, the current market price captures all information that might affect the price, even if that information is not generally known to the market. Of course,

---

[9] Stocks are often said to follow a "random walk," which means that there is no correlation between the price movement today and the price movement tomorrow. If there was a correlation between prices today and tomorrow, profit-seeking entrepreneurs could exploit the correlation and make low-risk profits.

[10] Using information not generally available to the market is known as insider trading. It is an offense to use inside information to trade in markets in both the U.S. and Canada. The latest big investor to fall afoul of U.S. insider trading legislation is Raj Rajaratnam, billionaire founder of the Galleon hedge fund, who was convicted of making $63 million in illegal trading profits. The complete story is found at: http://www.ft.com/intl/cms/s/0/a22a994a-71b0-11e0-9adf-00144feabdc0,dwp_uuid=64f9d27e-bcb8-11de-a7ec-00144feab49a.html#axzz1YFjnw5Dh

this would confer a huge advantage to those able to obtain and use inside information.

If Fama is correct and a market is at least semi-strong form efficient, an investor should be able to outperform the market in one of two ways. He or she must be either a better analyst of the information available to the market or he or she must have and make use of information the rest of the market does not have.

The EMH assumes that investors have rational expectations, that on average the population is correct (even if no one person is) and whenever new, relevant information appears, investors update their expectations appropriately. Note that it is not required that each investor be rational, as some investors may overreact and some may underreact to the news; it is the market as a whole is always right.[11]

For a time, the market's behaviour seemed to correlate well with the EMH and EMH dominated thinking. In the 1990s, however, a new group of thinkers arrived on the scene, suggesting that the market was driven not by rational expectations but by human emotions that had nothing to do with making smart, informed choices. This group of researchers, led by Nobel Laureate Daniel Kahneman and economist and author Richard Thaler, suggested that investors are subject to large errors in reasoning and information processing. These errors lead them to make predictable mistakes. This new area of study, known as "behavioural finance," has gained much traction in recent decades, as it appears to explain much of the apparently irrational behaviour that characterizes markets.

Back to Volatility

With the foregoing bits of theory to guide us, let's consider the following:

- First, why is volatility so high? Is it new information that is causing stock price indices to move by large amounts on an almost daily basis? Or is the constant flow of information feeding into something else, a more primal fear of what we don't know, or even what we don't know we don't know?
- Second, how do we position our portfolios to insulate them from the market's behaviour?

That investor par excellence, Warren Buffett, has often said that markets are driven by a combination of fear and greed. When risk appears low, greed takes over and prices rise as buyers rush in. When fear grips the market, investors head to the sidelines, selling as they go. Prices have to fall

---

[11] "Efficient-market Hypothesis," Wikipedia, found at: http://en.wikipedia.org/wiki/Efficient-market_hypothesis, accessed 16 November 2011.

sufficiently to induce someone else to buy, since no transaction can occur without a buyer on one side and a seller on the other side.

Before the 2008 meltdown, investors had come to believe that risk had largely disappeared from markets and markets were properly priced. This belief existed across the economic spectrum. Alan Greenspan, former chairman of the U.S. Federal Reserve and chief U.S. market regulator, often remarked that markets could regulate themselves better than an external regulator could. He accepted the widely held belief that markets had become so sophisticated in understanding and pricing risk that it was pointless for a regulator to challenge the collective wisdom of the market. If a bank became too highly leveraged, for example, market participants would discipline it by making it "pay up" to attract new deposit inflows. This would be enough to cause the bank to correct its behaviour. Because investors have a large stake in being right, and as regulators are always playing catch-up, the market would do a better job of policing market behaviour than a regulator.

Although the theory of market discipline sounds logical, reality has proven otherwise. The events unleashed in 2008 have made many investors realize that markets are not infallible and that even an institution as mighty as the Fed cannot save them from their mistakes. In this post-2008 environment, investors are very attuned to every new threat, whether real or imagined. A debt ceiling debate in the U.S. or problems with sovereign debt defaults in Europe are enough to make the markets roil with uncertainty. Underlying it all is the recognition that the entire developed world is awash in debt.

As the gravity of the situation seeps into the consciousness of investors everywhere, some stark realities cannot be avoided:

- Rising debt levels created an artificial stimulus that made both countries and individuals feel richer than they were. Just as debilitating, getting rid of debt will make people feel poorer than they are.
- How governments reduce their bloated levels of debt will affect everybody. All of the choices are painful and the pain will not be evenly spread. Governments have only four ways to lower debt: raise taxes, cut spending, inflate their way out of it, or default. The method(s) chosen will depend on the political power of the factions within society and will probably be some combination of all four.
- People in the Western world have come to expect a level of income and services that they cannot afford. When it comes time to pay the piper, this will cause increasing tension, especially in Europe, as citizens of the Mediterranean countries find their lifestyles

threatened. In the U.S., the growing inequality of personal incomes could escalate into social unrest, as it has in other parts of the world.

• Health care continues to consume an expanding share of GDP in many countries. Unless new ways of delivering and rationing health care are found, universal health care as we know it will cease to exist. This will become even more apparent as that demographic bulge, the baby boomers, head into their sixties and seventies over the next few decades.

What Can You Do to Recover?

• Pay down debt and remain liquid. Debt is one of the largest threats to your financial well-being. The risk-free return from eliminating consumer debt is often extremely high.

• Don't assume more risk than you are comfortable bearing. Equity markets are always risky. That risk is much higher in the post-2008 environment. Reduce your equity exposure to an amount with which you are comfortable. Chasing returns by assuming risk is not a good way to preserve and grow your wealth.

• Keep your equity investments well diversified. The world is a very uncertain place. Do not try to pick stocks, regions or even countries that will outperform, as events often move faster than investors. Eliminate the problem by diversifying the equity portion of the portfolio globally.

• Keep your fixed-income investments flexible with relatively short maturities. Interest rates are not going up any time soon, but eventually they will have to rise. When they do, long-maturity fixed-income investments will decline rapidly in value.

• High-risk fixed-income issues will fall in price (and rise in yield) much further and faster than low-risk issues.

PART 3

Real Wealth Management

CHAPTER 13

Recovery:
One Household at a Time

IN MID-2011, respected Canadian Finance Minister Jim Flaherty gave a stern warning. The words were simple, but direct:

Get your financial house in order.

It was good advice for the times: the credit worthiness of the United States had just suffered a significant blow and the downgrade of its rating from AAA to AA+ sent shivers of fear through global markets and into the hearts of panicked investors. But that was only the latest blow to a fragile global economy. Since 2008, crisis followed by crisis has slowed the painful convalescence of a world awash in debt.

So, what does it mean to get your fiscal house in order? If Japan, United States and Europe present risks that could send our recovery careening, if monetary policy is, indeed, ineffectual against a "balance sheet" recession, if the best minds in the world can't agree on how to resolve the situation in which we find ourselves, what can you — the individual investor — do?

There are steps you can take and that is the focus of this section of the book. You will gain insights on how to secure your family's financial health in the short term and how to reposition your financial activities to manage and control the outcomes you need in the long term. You will discover how to make use of what you can control, and ignore what you can't.

Financial Recovery in a Fragile Economy will introduce you to a framework around which you can use your financial resources to accumulate, grow, preserve and ultimately transition your accumulated wealth to the next generation with as much purchasing power as possible. It's called *Real Wealth Management.*™[1] It will help you understand how to use your money to your future advantage and how you can keep more of it by engaging in profitable relationships with professional advisors such as accountants, lawyers and financial advisors.

> *Real Wealth Management is a strategy for making the best decisions so you can accumulate, grow, preserve and transition sustainable family wealth with the most purchasing power possible after taxes, inflation and fees.*

Of course, you have to do your bit if you expect to benefit from Real Wealth Management. It requires a commitment to change your financial habits, especially if you are carrying too much debt. If you are under water financially, the baggage you have accumulated will weigh you down, even drown you. This chapter will address that by helping you understand how to create new money with tax and cost efficiency — so you can free yourself from the baggage of the past.

If debt is not a problem, perhaps navigating your investments through a volatile financial environment is. Change is difficult for everyone — individuals, organizations and global economies. Change, however, needs to be managed, and working closely with a professional team can keep you from making the wrong decisions and guide you to safe havens.

Yet, this is not about money alone. Financial recovery in a fragile world is about recovering peace of mind, knowing that you have accumulated enough to meet your basic needs and beyond that, so you have the luxury to choose the lifestyle you want.

> *Why is Real Wealth Management important? When you follow a strategic plan that encompasses all aspects of your financial life, you will increase your affluence, giving you freedom of choice.*

---

[1] Real Wealth Management™ is an interadvisory discipline pioneered and delivered by the Knowledge Bureau, a Canadian educational institute focused on professional development in tax and financial services. For more information, go to www.knowledgebureau.com.

How to Get Started

1. Pick your team. Your financial recovery will be greatly enhanced by taking a multiple-stakeholder approach to your convalescence.
2. In particular, with the right assistance, you can maximize the benefits of the tax system, as taxes substantively erode wealth, to turbo-charge emerging opportunities to increasing your income and capital over time.
3. More important, when you take a family approach to improving your financial affairs, you'll be leveraging the economic power of extended investment time horizons to build on your present strengths.

By taking a family focus, you will strengthen your financial health and that of the next generation, too.

A Strategy for Recovery

We live and invest in the aftermath of what Canada's government has called "the most synchronized recession in the post-war period. The ongoing financial market crisis is the worst since the Great Depression in the 1930s."[2]

If that is the case, what lessons can we learn from the Great Depression and its aftermath? Does it provide a methodical approach to financial recovery this time around? You bet. Let's look at annualized growth rates for the bellwether Dow Jones Industrial Average (DJIA), a proxy for the U.S. equities market.

- Had you invested a dollar on October 7, 1896, the first date for which annualized growth rates are published, and held it until mid-August 2011, the annual growth rate would have been **5.34%**.[3] That's interesting, because its 115-year timeline makes 5.34% a very reliable indicator of average annual growth.
- The Great Depression began with the stock market crash of October 29, 1929, known as "Black Tuesday." If you had invested a dollar that day and left it until mid-August 2011, your annualized growth rate would have been **4.86%**. Again, interesting, because it speaks to the consistency of the average annual return.

---

2 Canadian Federal Budget Papers, 27 January 2009.
3 "Annualized Growth Rates," found at: www.MeasuringWorth.com, accessed 2 November 2011.

- The largest recorded drop in the DJIA occurred on another dark day, October 19, 1987, or "Black Monday," when the index — and by proxy, investors — endured a one-day loss of **18.06%**. Had you invested a dollar that day and left it until mid-April 1998 — the peak of the next period of exhilaration — your annualized growth rate would have been **17.17%** for that eleven-year period.
- In that period of exhilaration, many investors dove into the market at the top, thinking it would just keep climbing higher. But it ended, beaten to death by the bursting of the tech bubble, a recession, the 9/11 terrorist attacks and SARS, which extended the length of the recession. A much different result was in store for those investors. If you had invested in mid-April 1998, at the peak, and held until December 31, 2007, just months before the 2008 financial crisis kicked off, you would have scored an annual growth rate of only **3.88%**.
- This is a much poorer result than you would have received if you had invested your dollar on October 6, 1931, the date of the largest one-day increase in the DJIA, when it increased 14.87%, If you left it there until mid-August 2011, your annualized return would have been **6.09%**.

(All of these returns, of course, are before taxes, inflation and the costs of investing.)

That is quite the range — from 3.88% to 17.17%, determined by something as happenstance as when you entered and exited the market. So, unless you have a crystal ball, you really can't bet the farm on what the market is going to do. If history tells us anything, it's this:

> *You can't count on the market to get yourself out of your present funk.*

Instead, suggests the senior deputy governor of the Bank of Canada, if you are to manage your financial recovery, you need to shift your focus:

> For the long-term investor, a fundamental shift is required, from thinking about a return target to considering appetite for risk and measuring and managing risk to the desired risk tolerance. The experience of the crisis provides some clear lessons for risk measurement and management and better communication.[4]

---

[4] Tiff Macklem, "Managing Risks in the New Economic Landscape," 27 September 2011.

By adopting a framework around which you build financial stability, you can better measure and manage risk and communicate with your family and advisors. Remember, the work of a financial survivor is recovery. No one can recover for you; the best your advisors can do is to keep you from hurting yourself more by helping you to manage risk. But, in the final analysis, it is up to you.

Real Wealth Management: It's for the Longer Term

In planning to build wealth that's sustainable over time — so important if you wish to position your family to weather future financial crises — you need a strategy, a process, a plan, and the right people to help you execute it.

With those supports in place, and by making decisions jointly with trusted advisors, you and your family can minimize your own negative financial behaviour. This will ensure that investment solutions align to financial objectives in accordance with your carefully constructed wealth-management plan, and that you are accountable for those decisions.

This is powerful because, now, investment-product solutions can be chosen, carefully and purposefully, according to defined benchmarks that have been set for the growth of the family's wealth using the economic forecasts at your disposal. Suddenly these forecasts are more meaningful, because the glimpses they provide into the future will allow you to plan your spending and savings decisions.

Because there are numerous skillsets required to execute a Real Wealth Management strategy properly — tax, investment and retirement-income planning, succession and estate planning — it is requires a multiple-advisor, interdisciplinary approach.

> *This is an interesting approach and an effective one because it's self-regulating. The various members of the advisory team must be in sync, working in tandem to execute the plan.*

To be sure the strategy is well executed, a number of professional advisors will be needed: accountants, lawyers and various financial specialists including insurance and investment advisors. All those with specialized service and investment product expertise must be on the same page, working to deliver solutions specific to the economic, financial and life events you are facing.

Can the average person put together this Real Wealth Management dream team? The short answer is "No." But the solution is in the recruitment of one trusted advisor who will assemble and manage the entire team. Whenever there is a group, leadership is required. So, find the one advisor whom you trust most — the one who knows you and your family best — and make him or her your leader. Then, together, you'll craft the strategic plan around which you will make your financial decisions and then you'll work with the team for the execution of those solutions.

What Can You Do to Recover?

- Manage debt. If high debt is your problem, you'll need a plan to get out of it — quickly. Unfortunately, governments can't help, but the right financial advisory team can coach you back to financial health.
- Manage risk. To better manage risk factors relating to the growth and preservation of your portfolio, rid yourself of the "fingers of instability" that plague your financial affairs. If you are unable to recover prior losses, you need to build up your strength. That requires a disciplined approach to savings.
- Make a strategic plan for recovery. The key to your successful financial recovery in a fragile world is to develop a plan, then follow it with discipline. Then you can achieve the long-term financial results you want.
- Find your trusted advisor, the one who knows your family best, the one who will lead your dream team of professional advisors. You have a lot of work ahead, so now is a good time to start.

CHAPTER 14

Taking Action: Tools of the Trade

BUILDING YOUR REAL WEALTH MANAGEMENT PLAN requires financial analysis. Three key financial documents will help you plan and measure your progress:

- **The personal net worth statement**, which is a snapshot of accumulated assets minus accumulated debt to show your net wealth;
- **The tax return**, which defines disposable income after taxes.
- **The financial plan**, which marries future decision-making about the creation of income and capital with solutions that are economically sound.

Let's take a look at each of them.

A Focus on Personal Net Worth

When you consider the state of your financial health, *you will talk about your personal and family net worth*. That's what gets measured over time: the financial stability of your financial balance sheet. That's important because when you better understand how financially stable you are, you'll be less likely to act irrationally when faced with fluctuations in the financial marketplace.

Statistics Canada's *Survey of Financial Security* uses the following and simple definition to describe net worth:

Net worth is the value of all assets less all debt. It's what you have left if you liquidated all your assets and paid off all your debt.[1]

The Net Worth Statement

Total Assets	Less	Total Debt	Equals	Net Worth
Private pension assets –RRSPs, RRIFs, LIRAs, Other –Employer Pension Plans		**Mortgages** –Principal residence –Other real estate		
Financial assets –Deposits in financial institutions –Mutual funds, investment funds, income trusts –Stocks –Bonds –Other financial assets		**Lines of credit** –Deductible –Non-deductible		
Non-financial assets –Principal residence –Other real estate –Vehicles –Other non-financial assets		**Credit card debt** **Installment debt**		
Equity in business		**Student loans**		
		Vehicle loans		
		Other debt		
TOTAL		**TOTAL**		$

The net worth statement is an interesting and informative document. It reflects equity that is accrued before taxes and after costs.

(Income, remember, is taxed when it's earned for tax purposes, but capital is taxed when you dispose of it. That's an important distinction if you are to understand planning for income versus capital. Together, income and capital contribute to building wealth, and your timing in generating both income and capital gains or losses is important to your overall wealth-building activities. You'll learn more about that later.)

---

[1] "The Wealth of Canadians," Statistics Canada, 2006

The personal net worth statement also details your liabilities or what you owe. That's important because your liabilities must be taken into account when you are making investment decisions. If debt levels are low compared to the value of your assets, you are well positioned to leverage your capital to build more wealth. If debt has accumulated, you will need to address those debt levels before you can leverage your capital and take advantage of wealth-building opportunities.

When we focus on personal and family net worth, we look at the whole picture, and that picture can be quite positive, in Canada at any rate.

In a report entitled *Summary Report on Retirement Income Adequacy Research*, Jack Mintz, research director and Palmer Chair in public policy, School of Public Policy, University of Calgary, had this to say about wealth accumulation in Canada:

> Household assets have generally been rising faster than their liabilities since the early 1990s, except for 2008 when financial market values sharply dipped. Household net worth was six times earnings in 2009 compared to four times earnings in 1970. The growth in assets and debt is influenced by a number of factors, especially demographic effects as people tend to save most in later parts of their careers — the populous baby boomers are now reaching retirement.[2]

Mintz also referenced a paper by James Davies of the economics department of the University of Western Ontario, entitled "Efficiency and Effectiveness of Savings Instruments Design:"[3]

> In the paper by Davies, a breakdown of assets and liabilities per household is provided for working and retired Canadians for 2005. He finds that on average, Canadians in retirement have $485,000 in net worth. The most important category is pension and tax-sheltered savings ($174,000 per household) although disposals of these assets are fully subject to taxes. The principal residence category is $152,000 per household but disposals are not taxed. Other financial, business and real estate assets at retirement are

2   Jack M. Mintz, *Summary Report on Retirement Income Adequacy Research*, Department of Finance Canada, 18 December 2009, found at: http://www.fin.gc.ca/activty/pubs/pension/riar-narr-eng.asp, accessed 3 November 2011.
3   James Davies, "Efficiency and Effectiveness of Savings Instruments Design," prepared for the Research Working Group on Retirement Income Adequacy, Department of Finance Canada, 3 December 2009, found at: http://www.fin.gc.ca/activty/pubs/pension/ref-bib/davies-eng.asp, accessed 3 November 2011.

$170,000 per household of which the income and capital gains from disposals are taxed. Retired Canadians have relatively low debt ($11,000 per household), about one-sixth of the level when working.[4]

These positive statistics continued into 2010, thanks to increasing real estate values; by year end, median personal net worth had risen to $181,000. But the volatility of 2011 brought with it predictions that currency fluctuations, inflation and more debt could dampened the growth in Canadians' net worth, particularly in 2012.

So, it is well worth it to build your personal net worth statement, and to monitor changes in it as you weather financial storms. It is central to understanding your financial health and stability. You may be in better shape than you think.

The Tax Return

The tax system is the first place to look for often-significant sums of money that can provide cash flow and help you manage debt in times of disaster recovery. The opportunities can be particularly powerful when your tax and financial advisors work together.

To begin, let's look at how to survive and thrive:

Don't delay paying Canada Revenue Agency (CRA) your balance due. You don't need trouble with the taxman anytime but especially not in turbulent economic times. If you have filed your return but still owe CRA money, some simple advice: clear it up — it's not going to go away. Taxpayers pay interest on their overdue balances at a prescribed annual rate that changes quarterly. As of the end of 2011, that rate was 5%.

Do file your income tax return. The ostrich approach doesn't work here, either. Clear up that delinquent tax return, as the interest clock will just keep ticking on any taxes due, including late-filing penalties and past interest accumulations, or worse, gross negligence or tax evasion penalties in severe cases. If cash flow problems are the reason for not filing, solicit the help of a tax advisor. He or she can speak to the tax department's collections division to arrange for you to make payments over time.

If you neglect to file your tax return and, indeed, you owe the CRA money, the tax department has the power to garnishee your wages — which will only make matters worse, right? Much more pleasant is the possibility that the taxman owes you money. Now that would be delightful; however, you must file a return to tap into it.

---

[4] Mintz, *Summary Report on Retirement Income Adequacy Research.*

If you have filed a return, but the CRA contests the amount you think is payable, be sure to file a "Notice of Objection." You must do so on the later of the following two dates:

- one year after the filing deadline for your tax return, or
- ninety days after the mailing date of the Notice of Assessment or Reassessment.

That will suspend collection activities for the amount in dispute, giving you some breathing room to sort out your tax affairs. However, this should be done only in conjunction with sound tax advice. Professional fees paid to dispute taxes you clearly owe will only exacerbate the problem, even though those fees are tax deductible.

Position yourself to tap into social benefits. When family net income falls below certain pre-determined levels, a family may receive social benefits, such as the Canada Child Tax Benefit, from the government. This won't happen until a tax return is filed, another reason to do so promptly, particularly if you have lost your job or your income has dropped for another reason. Likewise, Old Age Security (OAS) is subject to income testing; this time on an individual, rather than a family basis. Again, filing a tax return is very important if seniors are to maximize those benefits.

Don't cash in registered retirement savings plan (RRSP) deposits, if possible. Your creditors are pressuring you and you have to come up with some money fast. But cashing your RRSPs should be a last resort. This will simply cause a tax problem next year, and prolong your recovery cycle. Look for other sources to fund immediate bills, including CRA's refund recovery opportunity, explained below.

Review previously filed returns. You may correct errors and omissions on previously filed returns going back ten years. The result: the tax department will owe you money! But do get some help with this, as missed returns also cause incorrect balances in the contribution room for your RRSP and tax-free savings account (TFSA) — two very important investment opportunities you should maximize every year. You'll also miss out on properly reporting capital losses, which can help you recover taxes payable from the past or well into the future.

Claim your capital losses. Many people make the mistake of not claiming their stock market losses on their income tax returns. One reason is that they don't want their spouses to know. (That's bad on several fronts!) Another is that they think their losses have no tax value.

Although it's true that capital losses must be used against capital gains, in a year when you have no gains, those losses can be carried backward to offset capital gains reported in the previous three tax years, or carried forward indefinitely to offset future capital gains. If you never have another taxable capital gain as long as you live, capital losses can still be used to offset other income of the year of your death or the immediately preceding year. So they are very valuable throughout your entire tax-filing life.

If you have made this mistake in the past, correct it now. Remember, you can correct errors and omissions for up to ten years in the past. Then apply your unused losses against prior year gains. You may be in line for multiple-digit tax refunds. That will go a long way toward shoring up a margin call, if needed. Crystallizing losses during this recent spate of market volatility may not make sense otherwise.

The Financial Plan

Whereas your personal net worth statement measures your financial stability at a specific point in time (much as a balance sheet does for a business), the financial plan looks to the future. It is a projection of what your income and expenses will be at a future date, determined by a number of factors including your cash-flow projections, your budgeted expenses and the anticipated performance of your income-producing capital.

> *Key to effective financial planning is the ability to take into account all relevant aspects of your financial situation, and to identify and analyze the interrelationships among sometimes conflicting objectives.*[5]

The financial plan plots your financial journey to a specific financial destination, based on your age and timeframe, your goals and the money you have available. Think of it as planning for a trip; you begin by choosing your destination, you then establish your basic needs (shelter, transportation) and add in desired lifestyle activities along the way.

To continue the analogy, a quality financial plan will not only determine whether you'll be staying in a three-, four- or five-star hotel but will also pinpoint how much sight-seeing you can afford on your trip. It will also try to anticipate the unexpected: detours on your road to financial security, potholes that will slow you down, and severe weather that will throw you off course. And just as on a trip, when that happens, you will need to revisit your financial roadmap and revise your plan.

---

[5] Financial Planning Standards Council, found at: https://www.fpsc.ca/financialplanning/faqfinancialplanning, accessed 9 November 2011.

A financial plan will analyze the best way for you to allocate each dollar of income across the multiple objectives you may have both for the present and your future.

Using Your Money: Planning to Build Real Wealth

So, if a Real Wealth Management Plan requires a financial plan, as well as a personal net worth statement and income tax returns, where do you start? If you want a wealth strategy that your whole professional advisory team can buy into, start with your most trusted advisor, your key wealth manager, and plot your course.

The components: A successful Real Wealth Management Plan begins with a clear understanding of your net worth, then integrates personal, potentially life-changing events that could trigger action, and takes into account your recent financial behaviour. In other words, it considers your needs and wants and then analyzes after-tax income, liabilities and capital accumulations.

It then projects the need for income and capital to meet the four distinct requirements you have for your money:[6]

1. Non-discretionary spending
   - Basic needs, including food, clothing, shelter, utilities, transportation;
   - Taxes;
   - Debt management;
   - Incapacity and associated medical and home-care costs.
2. Discretionary spending
   - Emergency funds covering six months to one year of living expenses;
   - Savings for education and career advancement;
   - Savings for retirement and disability;
   - Risk management such as life and health insurance.
3. Income-producing capital
   - Accumulation of capital in registered and non-registered accounts;
   - Growth of capital by diversifying income sources and maximizing returns;
   - Preservation of capital by being tax efficient.

---

[6] As taught in the Elements of Real Wealth Management, published by Knowledge Bureau (2011).

4. Transitioning sustainable wealth
   • Preserve capital in your lifetime through tax-efficient transfers of assets;
   • Preserve capital at death through tax-efficient transfers.

Your Real Wealth Management Plan will be specific to your life cycle; it will be multi-faceted and, depending on your stage in life, will include the following:

• an investment plan,
• an education plan,
• a pre-retirement plan,
• a retirement income plan,
• a plan for disability, and
• an estate plan.

Ask your most trusted advisor and your professional advisory team to develop these plans and integrate them into your Real Wealth Management Plan. Your Real Wealth Management Plan will eliminate the eroding effects of taxes, inflation and fees and build future purchasing power, which will turbo-charge the value of your savings so you can accomplish your financial planning goals. Without this strategic plan, your financial plan is weak.

Then, even more important, refer to your plan often when making joint decisions with your advisory team. It is a great way for you to take control of your financial relationships. It is also a great way to keep your financial behaviour — and your advisors' behaviour — in check during times of volatility in the marketplace. If you build your strategic financial plan, then fail to follow it, that's a problem. You should either move on to a new advisory relationship or take leadership and initiate action.

What Can You Do to Recover?

• Create a Real Wealth Management Plan. Begin by analyzing your personal net worth statement and your income tax returns. The goal is to understand where you are now financially so you can position yourself to accumulate, grow, preserve and transition more of what you have in the future. Then, start building your financial plan for recovery. Real Wealth Management is about how well your investment, retirement, estate and tax planning work together over time.

• Break up the use of every dollar. Ensure that every dollar of available income and capital is spread across all four elements of Real Wealth Management: accumulation, growth, preservation and transition of wealth, in the most balanced manner. And make efficient use of your dollars: save "redundant" income; reduce taxes on income and capital dispositions; be vigilant about fees and choosing tax efficient investments.

- Find the right team. Many financial advisors are paid by commission and they focus on finding product solutions for you. That is a different service, one that comes later, after a full financial plan is designed as part of a long-term Real Wealth Management strategy. Real Wealth Managers will focus on building your net worth and the purchasing power your assets will produce over time. To recover properly in this fragile world, you need to work with the latter. Advisors holding the Master Financial Advisor (MFA)[7] designation are specifically trained in this discipline.

- Get your tax filings up to date and report all your capital losses. This will position you to recover gold from previously filed tax returns and increase TFSA and RRSP contribution room. Remember that contribution room is not indexed to inflation; using it sooner makes you richer. You may also qualify for social benefits and new tax credits if your income is less than income ceilings established for these purposes.

---

[7] The Master Financial Advisor designation is offered by the Knowledge Bureau, as is the Real Wealth Management Certificate Course, which may be taken by investors who wish to collaborate better with their advisory teams.

CHAPTER 15

Disaster Recovery: It's Family-Centred

HOW QUICKLY YOU RECOVER from uncertain economic times is directly related to the quality of your disaster recovery plan.

If you had a Real Wealth Management Plan when the crisis hit, a disaster recovery plan may be a moot point. In that case, you were probably prepared for the black swans of the day. But although you may have deflected most of the hits that came your way, it is likely your investment portfolio sustained some degree of damage.

If you didn't have a plan, you are no doubt in worse shape than before the recent volatility. You may be smothered by debt, reeling with losses and so traumatized you can't act rationally.

In both cases, your personal disaster recovery plan is a critical factor in a speedy recovery, especially because our world is likely to stay fragile for some time to come. But here is the good news: according to the principles of Real Wealth Management, you are not going through this alone. Your team of financial professionals can and will guide you through the process. Your family team should be involved, too. If you don't have a team supporting you, your first step to recovery is building your team.

In short, you don't have to recover from financial disaster alone. In fact, you shouldn't.

Past Disaster

When was the Great Depression over? Officially, in 1939, ten years after it began. Yet, just two years after the crash, on October 6, 1931, the bellwether Dow Jones Industrial Average (DJIA) recorded its largest one-day increase of 14.87%.[1] Imagine the exhilaration investors felt as they flocked back into an exuberant marketplace.

Unfortunately, it was only a brief reprieve. The full brunt of the crash soon trickled down to the people on the ground and demolished a decade. Investments held from October 29, 1929, to January 1, 1939, fared poorly; the DJIA **lost** 4.64% each year of that decade, making a one-day gain of 14.87% irrelevant in the long term.

It was all the worse because, before the Crash, many individuals had paid for their extravagant lifestyles using credit; after the crash, credit disappeared and those individuals had no savings on which to fall back. Then, when people stopped buying in order to pay off their debts and start saving, businesses failed. Jobs were lost, consumption dried up even more, more businesses failed. Banks failed.

Does any of this sound familiar?

In mid 2011, around the time the U.S. government's credit rating was downgraded because of its debt, 72% of Canadians owed money; 40% were unprepared to handle their financial obligations in the event of an emergency and 26% had less than three months savings in case of a disaster such as a job loss or disability.[2]

So, where does that leave us? With this much debt, Canadians every day abdicate their purchasing power to their creditors. That, of course, makes you poorer faster.

And it is not as if Canadians are forsaking debt in the face of economic uncertainty. Newspapers report investors willing to take on additional debt — through margin accounts, investment loans and home equity loans — to take advantage of volatile markets.[3] But those same investors are just as likely to sell their investments at a loss when markets fluctuate wildly. Unfortunately, we humans seem to have an unerring knack for doing the wrong things at the wrong times.

---

[1] "Annualized Growth Rates," found at: www.MeasuringWorth.com.

[2] Harris/Decima Poll conducted for CIBC, summer 2011.

[3] Ray Turchansky, "Debt-ceiling deal in US has investors pondering their next moves," *Post Media News*, 13 August 2011.

*Individual investors, in fact, do exactly the wrong things at the
most volatile times.*

It is as if we can't process good news when in a state of panic or
prolonged shock. For example, a strong economic forecast for the five
years ahead is all but meaningless if today we are rattled by events. We like
to feel we are in control: we feel as if we must act now, even if this hurts us
in the future, even if we know better. We become more agitated by what we
have already experienced (loss, in this case) than by market forecasts of
what our future experience will be.[4]

*Individual investors lose money in times of great volatility
because this is the precise time they want to change their path
and trade against their advisor's advice, thereby causing great
damage to their portfolios.*

How much damage? Staggering damage. A large-scale study done in
Taiwan (Taiwan has the world's twelfth largest financial market) analyzed
the activities of do-it-yourself investors from 1995-1999, relatively good
years in financial market terms.[5] The losses to individual investors from
active trading tallied about 2% of Taiwan's GDP. Staggering, indeed!

*Investors would have been better off financially to put their
money under their mattress than to trade on their own accounts.*

The moral of the story: if you work closely with your professional
advisors during volatile times, allowing the advisors to help you manage
your financial behavior, you will get better results. In fact, some argue that
the best an investor can do in fragile times is to assemble a low-cost, well-
diversified, tax-efficient portfolio, then let his or her professional financial
advisors keep him or her from trying to outperform the market by trading
every time the landscape changes.

---

4 Philip Z. Maymin and Gregg S. Fisher, "Preventing Emotional Investing: An Added Value
   of an Investment Advisor," *Journal of Wealth Management,* Spring 2011, found at: www.
   iinews.com/site/pdfs/JWM_Spring_2011_GersteinFisher.pdf, accessed 7 November 2011.
5 Brad M. Barber, Yⁿ-Tsung Lee, Yu-Jane Liu and Terrance Odean, "Just How Much Do Individual Investors Lose by Trading?" *Review of Financial Studies,* vol. 22, no. 2 (2009), pp. 609-632.

*That, in fact, is the key role of your financial advisors: to stop
excessive trading responses that will significantly erode your
wealth in volatile times.*

*Wealth advisors take note: this forced discipline is highly valued
by the individual investor.[6]*

Triage: Working with Your Recovery Team

Before checking your ailing financial affairs into the "emergency room" of
your financial advisory team, be ready for triage from your team members.
Financial triage follows a process similar to that of an emergency room or
a MASH unit. Look up the term "triage" in the *Merriam Webster Dictionary*
and you'll find this definition, which provides useful context to financial
disaster survivors:

> *Triage: the assigning of priority order to projects on the basis of
> where funds and other resources can best be used, are most needed,
> or are most likely to achieve success.*

In assessing your financial damage, you need to consider three
questions:
1. How critical is my financial wound?
2. What's my financial history?
3. How do we contain the damage in the current environment?

How critical is my financial wound? Are you going to lose your house,
your job, your health? Or, do you simply need a coping mechanism for the
fear and anxiety you feel in today's market conditions as your digest the
diminished value of your investment portfolio or retirement savings?

In the first instance, you need to act quickly to stop the bleeding; you'll
move to the front of the line. In the second, the priorities are different. You
can afford to wait, but you'll need to understand how to contain the damage
short term. You may require no further treatment, just ongoing support to
make sure you don't cause yourself further harm while you rehabilitate the
financial wounds.

What's my financial history? To assess your financial stability, your
advisors need to complete and analyze your financial documents. Be
prepared to bring along your Net Worth Statement, your tax returns and
the financial plans you hopefully have constructed with your advisors in

---

[6] Maymin and Fisher, "Preventing Emotional Investing: An Added Value of an Investment
Advisor."

the past. Your advisory team will want to consider how to improve your after-tax cash flow, in order to meet new investment objectives.

How do we contain the damage? The support of family members can greatly advance recoveries. This is true of financial recoveries, as well. Yet, many families don't talk to each other about money. It's a taboo subject, according to recent studies about the communications baby boomers have with their offspring:[7]

- Almost 50% of boomers think their children will not have the financial maturity to handle inheritances until those children reach age thirty-five.
- About 50% of boomers have not told their children how much money they have.
- 15% have disclosed nothing about family wealth.

And although 84% of parents believe their children would benefit from discussions with a financial professional, 60% have never introduced their children to their advisors. There is much work to be done to bring the family up to speed, especially when the family's finances are in recovery.

Sharing your beliefs about the use of your money, now and in the future, is an important life skill. But sharing can be difficult if you have never talked to your family about money in the past. Financial plans are often thwarted because family members are not in sync with financial values. The Real Wealth Management process can help.

Your Two Teams

Your most trusted advisor is at the centre of your financial well being. He or she is your financial educator, advocate and financial steward, all wrapped up into one. This is the captain of your ship, overseeing the actions of all the members of your advisory team. He or she will manage the financial documentation — net worth, tax returns and financial plans — and share them, as you permit, with the other advisors.

This person will have a deep knowledge of all the financial and life planning issues for you and your family, and will initiate and explain the components of the Real Wealth Management Strategic Plan.

But, in order to accumulate, grow, preserve and transition wealth on an intergenerational basis, a strategic plan must be built so that both the family team and the advisory team can follow it. Your family team includes those in your inner circle. They are the stakeholders who will benefit from a Real Wealth Management strategy and plan. They are the people to whom

---

[7] "Baby Boomers," Spectrem Group, Chicago, March 2011.

you will eventually transfer your family wealth, and with whom you may wish to do some income splitting for tax purposes.

These stakeholders need to know about the consequences of your financial recovery and any resulting changes in spending and savings. Once you have pulled both sides together, you are positioned to begin your financial recovery.

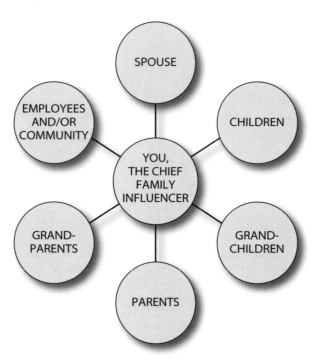

By inviting your family members to discuss their financial concerns, you can have a better discussion about the financial triggers that affect the whole family, achieving buy-in on important decisions that have to be made. By framing discussion around a simple checklist, you can and your family can share our visions and develop values and objectives for moving forward:

Client Action Triggers Checklist[8]

Life Triggers: Based on your age and the age of your spouse, discuss the milestones that concern you:
- Education
- Independent living
- First job
- Marriage
- Baby
- Illness
- Loss of work or business
- Separation or divorce
- Retirement
- Death of a loved one

Financial triggers: What specific financial concerns do you have?
- Funding basic "needs"
- Funding "wants" now and/or in the future
- Cash flow: when expenses outdistance income
- New savings opportunities
- Taxes and plans for avoiding or deferring

Economic triggers: What are you hearing on the news? Do you understand how this affects you?
- Market and portfolio losses
- Inflation
- Interest rates
- Currency valuations
- Fees for investment services
- Advisor fraud and trust issues

By fleshing out and discussing these concerns, your family is well positioned to move together on the road to financial recovery.
- Which objectives must be met to recover in the short term?
- What does your family net worth statement tell you about your financial stability?
- Can benefits of the tax system help you increase cash flow or pay down debt?
- Would family income splitting help reduce tax burdens and create new money?
- How can tax-efficient asset transfers preserve wealth now and at death?

---

8   The Action Triggers Checklist is a component of Real Wealth Management, as taught in the certificate courses of the Knowledge Bureau.

What Can You Do to Recover?

- Find a most trusted financial advisor who will answer your most pressing "trigger questions" about life events, financial events and economic events. This is the first step in the Real Wealth Management process. Listen carefully for the quality of the answers. You are looking for a highly competent technician from a product knowledge point of view, but you are also looking for an educator, an advocate and a steward for your money.
- Initiate a team meeting. Working with a team of financial experts in the area of tax, investment, retirement, insurance or estate planning is your first line of defence in assessing and correcting the damage you have sustained in the financial crisis. Each can play a significant role in your financial recovery. Further, they can keep the other in check, working toward the same strategic Real Wealth Management Plan.

  Use trigger questions to interview your advisory team. Formulate your most pressing trigger questions, then use them as an "interview questionnaire" when meeting your team of advisory professionals. It's a smart way to weed out advisors with whom you do not want to work.
- Invite the family into the fray. Families working together have the potential to conjoin their individual economic power to become economic powerhouses. Those who are financially estranged miss an opportunity to leverage the potential of proper tax, investment, retirement and estate planning. Make sure the right stakeholders are invited to the "financial triage" meeting.
- Verbalize your vision and values. What would you like to accomplish and how? When you think about the future, what is your financial vision and values? Both your family and your advisory team should understand your vision and values — your advisory team because it will build the appropriate benchmarks and rules for accumulation, growth, preservation and transition of wealth that reflect your risk tolerance; your family because they will support you.

Now you should be ready to work with your financial recovery team on your disaster recovery plan.

CHAPTER 16

Financial Maturity and Responsible Decision-Making

WHAT'S YOUR OPERATING LINE? How much more money does it take each month to cover your expenses than you bring in? How much should you be spending on those little luxuries each month? More important yet, how much money do you save each month?

In an electronic world, many people don't understand their cash inflows and outflows — except that everything that flows in seems to flow out just as rapidly! Cash flow is one of those concepts that alludes many people's grasp; they simply don't understand *why* there is nothing left for savings at the end of the month.

Another concept that confuses many individuals is the exact amount of their pre-tax and after-tax income. How is it you can negotiate a great pay with your employer, only to be caught by complete surprise when the amount electronically deposited in your account bears no resemblance to what you agreed upon? In fact, there is a gaping discrepancy. Often, the difference is taxes and the mandatory withholdings for pensions and benefits that you failed to take into account. Your gross pay is pre-taxes, your net pay is after taxes.

To build financial stability and recover ground in a fragile financial world, you need to know the exact amount in each case. When you do, you are on the road to understanding how you use your money to your long-term advantage.

Financial Maturity:
Understanding How You Use Your Money

So, what does it matter how you use your money? After all, it's your money. But, are you really in control of it? You may be abdicating too many dollars to the taxman, and making unhealthy choices, such as taking on too much credit card or mortgage debt.

Your financial recovery begins with knowing where your money goes. When you do, you will understand how to "patch the gaps" and plan for your future financial well-being. In addition, you and your tax and financial advisors can discuss positive ways to change your financial behaviour, if required.

For example, we all know people who make lots of money but barely cover non-discretionary expenditures such as food, clothing and shelter. These folks may be bringing in loads of cash, but they have few financial skills. They don't know the difference between "needs" and "wants" — and that stops them from building and preserving wealth.

We determine "*financial maturity*" by where you are in the four stages in the use of money:

1. **Non-discretionary spending:** This is money you spend for the basic necessities—food, clothing, shelter, transportation, medical costs and servicing debt. We add in the latter because financial stability can depend on making sure creditors (especially powerful Canada Revenue Agency) do not garnishee wages or make calls on margin accounts.

    Basic living expenses should never eat up the entire family budget. Yet, often because of the pressure people feel to "keep up with the Joneses," a pattern of buying larger homes and all the toys has consumed Canadian families. A "basic" lifestyle is not so basic anymore; certain lifestyle choices are now considered "non-discretionary" when, in fact, they are completely discretionary.

    Disciplined spending on what you define as basic needs provides room for the next category of spending, which is critical to your ability to survive a financial crisis. The fine line between the two — non-discretionary and discretionary spending — demands fresh thinking if you want to ensure you have enough for basic needs now and in the future.

2. **Discretionary spending:** The choices that people make today concerning their needs and wants (big house, expensive car, glamorous travel) affect their ability to finance their future needs. Many of us know we should save for our retirement, for example,

but it's so far in the future, it's easy to put it aside in favour of buying something more tangible in the present. But what would you do if you lost your job in the aftermath of the global financial crisis? What if you lost it next week?

Needs *must* be financed with current dollars; wants *should be* financed with savings. In other words, needs require a "present orientation" and wants a "future orientation." Too much of a present orientation makes you prone to undisciplined impulse spending. When we carefully spend money today with a view to securing enough for our future, we can be left with "redundant income" that can be saved, first for emergencies (six months to one year of income), then for education (which boosts earning ability and creates the opportunity to increase net worth) and, finally, for retirement income security.

Once you have looked after your future income needs, by all means, go on a lovely vacation and budget for those shoes you've been eying! You deserve it, because you have used your money responsibly.

3. **Building income-producing capital:** People who have enough to meet needs now and in the future, get to this stage: they can use their money as an income-producing tool. In other words, they regularly save it, then forget about it. They neither need it nor want it now. Its purpose is to grow for the future and its strength will be determined by its purchasing power in the future.

   That means the income this capital produces — interest, dividends, rents or royalties — needs to be free from the eroding effects of taxes and inflation, so that it can grow and buy the lifestyle you want for yourself and your heirs.

   You also want to be sure your investment income is not being eaten by exorbitant interest charges, management expense ratios and other investment fees. This requires a smart investment strategy and a team of advisors who are focused on the right solutions — before and after taxes — to build and grow your capital, no matter what the global economic cycle brings in this fragile recovery period. In fact, when returns on your investments are low or even nil, a tax focus can add double-digit returns to your investments. So can a vigilance around the cost of investing. Your advisors need to be on top of this — and you need to ask about it.

4. **Preserving sustainable wealth.** You have taken care that taxes, inflation and fees are not eroding the value of your capital now and

in the future. Disciplined investors apply that same vigilance when they dispose of their income-producing capital, whether it be by sale, transfer or at death. Any changes in the value of your assets are "realized" for tax purposes when those assets are sold, and are taxed accordingly. Likewise, when assets are transferred either before or upon death, there is a "deemed disposition" at "fair market value," which treats the transfer as if it were a sale and accrued values are taxed. There is one exception: if you are married, the rollover of assets to the surviving spouse may be tax-free.

Those who use their money most astutely in this stage understand that *when* they sell or transfer assets is crucial because it crystallizes wealth for tax purposes. They also understand the opportunities that realizing capital gains affords at the right time in an economic cycle, and how to avoid unwelcome taxes according to an overall wealth-management plan.

When your financial advisor determines what stage you are at in using your money, individually and as a family, he or she can develop a Real Wealth Management Plan that will move you toward financial stability today and sustain your wealth from one stage in your life to the next.

That plan must include tax efficiencies with strategies including family income splitting, tax deferrals and the transfer of assets into the proper hands at the right time — to keep more wealth in the family's hands and out of the taxman's pockets. That's a great way to recover financially in a fragile world. It also prepares you, with a great financial recovery plan, for the future.

Responsible Decision-Making

The Real Wealth Management Plan is the document that pulls together all the expertise and skills of your professional advisory team in a common, client-centred strategy. It is the document from which all stakeholders—family members and each member of your advisory team —make decisions about your financial well-being.

From a macro point of view the Real Wealth Management Plan integrates the economic forecasts of the day with the objectives of the family in such a way so as to put the family in control of its own financial destiny.

The Real Wealth Management approach also sets goals and establishes ways to measure your progress toward those goals; it sets standards for the collaborative process that will move you toward your goals; and, it has an evaluation and selection process for determining product solutions—from investment accounts to insurance to tax return preparation — that will take you safely to your goals. Just as important, it keeps these standards in place over time.

By its very nature, it provides the principles and rules by which your advisors will demonstrate professionalism, leadership, knowledge and trust as it relates to the strategic plan and, ultimately, to product selection. These are also the principles and rules you'll pass along to your proxies and heirs when the time comes.

At its essence, the Real Wealth Management Plan is a process that gives advisors and individuals a roadmap so they can make more responsible decisions about the family's wealth and achieve desired results — no matter what the global economic cycle forces upon you in the short term.

But if you are to accumulate, grow, preserve and transition wealth with purchasing power, it's important that everyone collaborates. As the wealth of the family grows, there is a risk that an individual member of the advisory team will take a "silo" approach and act independently of the overall Real Wealth Management Plan. Failing to act in concert will put the plan at risk, thwart disaster recovery plans and worse, do irreparable harm if potential "fingers of instability" are not identified.

The outcome: Your planning work in the Real Wealth Management process will have a natural outcome: joint decision-making within a specific strategy and using specific product solutions. And, because the Real Wealth Management Plan is matched to your interests, motivations and values, you can relate to the plan on an emotional level. That takes reactive financial behaviour out of the picture. You can handle market volatility because you are employing your most trusted advisor in the most important role: keeping you from making reactive decisions that can erode your wealth.

What Can You Do to Recover?

- Define the difference between wants and needs. If you are going to move on to the next stage, you need to save and accumulate income-producing capital. This is the first step.
- Re-prioritize spending and savings. By better understanding how you use your money, you'll be able to allocate resources according to your personal milestones, and you'll build sustainable wealth.
- With the participation of family and your professional advisory team, **build** on your Real Wealth Management Plan. Your Real Wealth Management plan will **continue** to deliver wealth accumulation **opportunities**.
- Within the framework of your plan, make responsible decisions — so you will arrive safely at your financial destination.

CHAPTER 17

Tax Efficiency: Part of a Real Wealth Management™ Plan

WHAT IS TAX EFFICIENCY? It is the process of arranging financial affairs within the framework of the law to pay the least possible taxes on income and the increasing value of income-producing assets, thereby enabling the continued accumulation, growth, preservation and transition of capital. This process ensures that a family's wealth grows, intact, with future purchasing power.

Tax efficiency is the prerequisite for sustainable family wealth. In the short term, it will increase your family's cash flow. In the medium term, it will enhance your investment returns. In the long term, it will protect family net worth from erosion.

The problem with taxes in general is it's difficult to be an expert at something you do only once a year. Yet, expertise is exactly what is required if you are going to protect your money from the eroding effects of the sizeable federal and regional taxes you will pay throughout your lifetime. Tax efficiency is critical, too, if you plan to count on your savings in retirement, when actively earned income stops. In this regard, working with a team of professional advisors who understand how to protect your money from tax erosion can really pay off.

Financial advisors should focus just as much time on the tax efficiency of their clients' income, says Master Your Retirement *author and Real Wealth Manager Douglas Nelson, as they do on their clients' capital.*[1]

A taxpayer's "marginal tax rate" is a useful tool for measuring tax-efficiency of both actively and passively earned income. Your marginal tax rate will tell you how much taxes you'll pay on the next dollar you earn, while measuring the effect of that income on your eligibility for tax credits and social benefits delivered through the tax system. To compute it, you need to understand that, for tax purposes, your income will be classified into several broad categories based on its source. For example:

1. **Ordinary income** includes income from employment, pension income and interest earned on your investments. It may also include alimony, income from social benefits such as Employment Insurance and net rental income (that is, what's left after allowable deductions). Ordinary income is added to taxable income in full.

2. **Income from self-employment** is net business income after allowable deductions have been subtracted from revenues.

3. **Capital gains** (or losses) reflect the increases (or decreases) in the cost base of your income-producing assets and, for tax purposes, these changes in value are realized on the disposition (sale or transfer) of the assets. Only half those gains, net of losses, are reported on your personal income tax return. Sometimes, gains can be avoided if, for example, certain properties are transferred to your favorite charity. Other gains may qualify for specific exemptions such as the $750,000 Capital Gains Exemption.

4. **Dividends** are the after-tax distribution of profits from private or public corporations to shareholders. Reporting them involves an integration of the corporate and personal tax systems, the end result of which is a preferential tax rate.

Knowing your marginal tax rate on your various income sources allows you to make informed choices about when to realize income for tax purposes, so you get the best after-tax results. The table below shows the combined federal and provincial marginal tax rates for four types of income. You can easily see the advantages of having income from a variety of sources, realized within various tax brackets: it strategically averages down the taxes you pay.

---

[1] Douglas Nelson, *Master Your Retirement: How to fulfill your dreams with peace of mind* (Winnipeg: Knowledge Bureau, 2012).

Marginal tax rates do vary by province, as illustrated by three provinces shown below:[2]

Canadian Federal and Provincial Marginal Tax Rates for 2011

Prov.	Taxable income range ($)	Ordinary income (%)	Capital gains (%)	Small corp. dividends (%)	Eligible dividends (%)
BC	Up to 10,527	0	0	0	0
	10,528 to 11,088	15.00	7.50	2.08	-2.03
	11,089 to 36,146	20.06	10.03	4.16	-9.43
	36,147 to 41,544	22.70	11.35	7.46	-5.70
	41,545 to 72,294	29.70	14.85	16.21	4.17
	72,295 to 83,001	32.50	16.25	19.71	8.11
	83,002 to 83,088	34.29	17.15	21.95	10.64
	83,089 to 100,787	38.29	19.15	26.95	16.28
	100,788 to 128,800	40.70	20.35	29.96	19.68
	More than 128,800	43.70	21.85	33.71	23.91
AB	Up to 10,527	0	0	0	0
	10,528 to 16,977	15.00	7.50	2.08	-2.02
	16,978 to 41,544	25.00	12.50	10.21	-2.02
	41,545 to 83,088	32.00	16.00	18.96	7.85
	83,089 to 128,800	36.00	18.00	23.96	13.49
	More than 128,800	39.00	19.50	27.71	17.72
ON	Up to 10,527	0	0	0	0
	10,528 to 37,774	20.05	10.03	2.77	-3.93
	37,775 to 41,544	24.15	12.08	7.90	1.85
	41,545 to 66,514	31.15	15.58	16.65	11.72
	66,515 to 75,540	32.98	16.49	17.81	12.49
	75,541 to 78,361	35.39	17.70	20.82	15.90
	78,362 to 83,088	39.41	19.70	23.82	18.32
	83,089 to 128,800	43.41	21.70	28.82	23.96
	More than 128,800	46.41	23.20	32.57	28.19

Source: EverGreen Explanatory Notes, Knowledge Bureau.

Combing the federal and provincial tax rates provides a quick way to determine the marginal tax rate for different income sources, but it has its drawbacks. It does not take into account "clawback zones" or provincial surtaxes.

---

[2] Updates are posted regularly in EverGreen Explanatory Notes and Knowledge Bureau Report, found at www.knowledgebureau.com. Also see Evelyn Jacks, *Essential Tax Facts* Winnipeg: Knowledge Bureau, 2011).

- **A clawback** refers to a reduction of a refundable or non-refundable tax credit or other social benefit when the taxpayer's income has risen above a certain ceiling. (The ceiling differs, depending on the benefit). Because of the progressive nature of our tax system — that is, the more money you earn, the more taxes you pay and the less income redistribution you qualify for — the effect of a clawback is an increased marginal tax rate.
- **A surtax** is a tax on a tax. This sometimes applies when income has risen to a certain level; it's a tax on those who earn enough to pay taxes.

It is important, therefore, to understand your marginal tax rate as it relates to the tax bracket into which your income falls, plus any resulting clawback of social benefits for which you may qualify. You'll also want to keep tabs on the imposition of surtaxes and other provincial variations to which you are subject so you understand the true value of your after-tax dollars. More important, you'll want to have a clear understanding of how much purchasing power — after taxes — the next dollar of income you earn will have. This generally requires the help of tax software and/or a tax accountant who can prepare the calculations for you.

Understanding both your marginal tax rate and your eligibility for various tax benefits is an effective tool in determining whether it's worthwhile for you to earn more of the same type of income or whether you should diversify your income sources for tax purposes. For example, you may wish to increase your tax efficiency by splitting income with family members or by realizing different income sources in different tax years. This is a conversation to have with both your tax and investment advisors present.

A contribution to a registered retirement savings plan (RRSP), for example, will reduce your net income, the figure used to determine any clawbacks of tax credits and social benefits, as well as your taxable income, the figure which determines federal and provincial tax rates and surtaxes. Understanding the impact of a contribution to an RRSP on your tax filing will allow you to do some tax planning to build real wealth — adding double-digit returns to that investment decision with marginal tax savings.

Samuel's RRSP Contribution

To demonstrate how effective this can be, consider Samuel, an Ontario father whose combined federal/provincial marginal tax rate is 43%. Samuel contributes $100 to his RRSP and his tax practitioner computes a tax benefit of $43. Samuel's refund on that year's tax filing will increase by

$43 — and his taxable income will go down by $43. That also means his family's Child Tax Benefit will increase by $4.

In other words, Samuel receives a 47% return on every dollar invested in his RRSP by way of reduced taxes and increased benefits — and that's before taking into account the tax-sheltered compounding of investment earnings within the RRSP. That's a great return on your investment by any standards.

With tax efficiency as a central focus of his planning, Samuel not only increases his capital accumulations within the RRSP but he also increases the future income his RRSP generates. As well, next year, his monthly cash flow increases, thanks to the increase in his monthly Child Tax Benefit.

Your tax advisor can no doubt provide more examples. They all add up to tax efficiency and more money saved, which contributes to the accumulation and growth of your wealth.

Tax Rules

High level, here are the basic tax rules you need to know to thrive in a fragile world:

- **Avoid paying taxes legally but avoid tax evasion.** It's your legal right and duty to arrange your affairs to pay the least taxes possible within the framework of the law. When making investment decisions, therefore, talk taxes first. If you bring a tax focus to your financial affairs, you will probably increase your returns by double-digits amounts.

    Tax evasion is a different kettle of fish. It is the deliberate understatement of income or overstatement of deductions or credit entitlements. And that is a no-no. If you voluntarily correct those errors (that is, tell the taxman about them before he tells you), you'll save yourself gross negligence and tax evasion penalties and, in severe cases, jail.

- **Use the economic power of the family unit.** Tax systems are indeed complicated, but they are chocked full of provisions that allow for tax savings using the economic power of the family unit. For example, consider:
    - income splitting,
    - the transfer of deductions and credits amongst family members, and
    - planning the tax-efficient transfer of assets, often in a tax-free or tax-reduced manner.

Each has specific rules to follow if your are to be onside with the tax department, but bottom line: you can and should use these opportunities to your advantage. They can save you thousands of dollars this year and tens of thousands of dollars over succeeding years. When it comes to taxes, it's not about you: the family that files together wins.

- **Use your tax refund to pay down debt.** The tax return is often an uncommitted source of new cash and you can use it to reduce debt. When you get your tax refund or recover overpaid taxes or past credits, use the money wisely: first pay down non-deductible debt such as credit cards and mortgages.
- **Deleverage by leveraging your tax advantages.** You can work toward increasing future tax refunds by leveraging your current one. Invest your refund in one of a variety of tax-assisted savings plans, such as an RRSP, a Tax Free Savings Account (TFSA) and the Registered Education Savings Plan (RESP) for your children. The RRSP is particularly important for the creation of new money from social benefits and tax credits, as we explained above. For every dollar you invest, you could receive double-digit returns, depending on your marginal tax rate. Now you can pay down bad debt with your savings.
- **Keep more of the first dollar you earn.** Don't overpay your taxes at source. Most people do because they receive a tax refund. Your goal is to pay only the correct amount of taxes at source, that is, make sure the taxes deducted from your pay cheque are correct, and not in excess of the taxes you are required to pay for the year. Also, don't prepay more than necessary if you pay your taxes by instalments. The best-laid plans for your investment portfolio will be scuttled if you take the money out prematurely to prepay taxes that will be refunded a year later. Remember: the government doesn't pay you for the use of your money. Usually the market does, even if you don't always get the returns you want.
- **Increase productivity: income sources attract different tax results**. Do understand how much money you will pay on the next unsheltered dollar you earn. Interest, dividends and capital gains all attract different marginal tax rates. Investing in a registered account, meanwhile, shelters your capital from tax erosion over time. Even your province of residence will influence your marginal tax rates. Take a look, because your income is taxed for the whole year based on your province of residence as of December 31. If moving to a higher-taxed province is in your future, do so at the start of next year, as a way of preserving more of this year's income.

- **Make wise choices: rethink your consumer impulses.** Buying any consumer item is very expensive when you consider it from a tax-efficiency perspective. Let's start with your employment income. You work hard for your money, but before you can use any of it, the taxman has already taken double-digit amounts[3] off your employment income in the form of personal income taxes. So, you start your shopping spree with diminished dollars: for average singles, for example, each dollar is worth only 70¢. Another way to look at this is that the first 2.25 hours in your 7.5-hour day is spent working for the government. Then you pay sales taxes.

  Consider that cute pair of shoes you simply must have. Depending on where you live in Canada, GST/HST/PST may add 5%-15% in sales taxes to your $100 price tag. Countries around the world are not exempt, either: value-added taxes in the vicinity of 20% are common in central Europe, for example.

  Then, if you pay for those shoes with your credit card and don't pay off your credit card at the end of the month, you can find yourself paying 20% or more in additional interest costs for that privilege.

  Add it all up and *that $100 pair of shoes could really be costing you $165.* That's a 65% premium on the first dollar you earned this morning. Is it worth it? At what point is it simply too expensive?

If nothing else does the trick, tax erosion from various sources should force you to think very carefully about the additional cost of your consumerism, at the expense of your future financial stability.

Financial Recovery: Stop the Bleeding

Worrying about the returns on our investments — or lack thereof — has caused us so much stress of late. We have spent much time discussing the financially fragile world and how the world got itself into this situation. Yet, at a personal level, we often choose to allow taxes and consumerism to eat away at our precious financial resources.

There is not much we can do to control the macro problems of global economies. In fact, at a more micro level, we don't have a whole lot more control; think of the sales or excise taxes we must pay.

But we can arrange our personal affairs within the framework of the law to pay less personal income taxes. We can also refuse to pay too much for consumer goods, credit card debt and depreciating assets. Those

---

[3] Organization for Economic Cooperation and Development, 2005 data. Singles in Canada pay an average personal income tax rate of 31.6%, including social security contributions paid by their employers; married couples with two children will pay an average of 21.5%.

expenditures do nothing to help us accumulate, grow, preserve and transition our money to achieve a more secure financial future.

Taxes and inflation will do a very good job of eroding the value of your hard-earned money. There is much you can do, however, to push back and manage both your after-tax cash flow and your tax-efficient investments so you maximize any government benefits and the tax preferences to which you are entitled. That's just smart, because it gives you more money today with which to prepare for your financial future. You'll pay less for those cute shoes, too.

Measuring your income or capital before taxes and inflation can exaggerate your financial stability. You want your savings to be strong and intact, fully able to replace the income you make today at that point in the future when you no longer have active income. How big does your personal net worth — that is, total net assets less taxes, inflation and debt — need to be for that to happen?

Financial recovery in a fragile world is about managing your purchasing power by eliminating those things that will erode your wealth, so you can be ready for the future, no matter how uncertain that may look today.

What Can You Do to Recover?

- Understand marginal tax rates and their impact on your ability to be tax efficient.
- Explore with your financial advisory team the economic power of the family unit; integrate tax-efficient strategies such as income splitting into your Real Wealth Management Plan.
- Use your tax refund to invest in your future, either by paying down debt or putting your refund into a tax-assisted savings plan.
- Rethink consumer purchases and the impact various layers of taxes can have on the real price of your purchases.
- Understand the demands of cash flow so you can access more of your cash when you need it.
- If you are concerned that the returns on your investments are insufficient after taking into account taxes and inflation, challenge your advisors to revisit your Real Wealth Management Plan. Can you reduce fees? Can you more effectively diversify your portfolio? Can you save money on your income tax return? Can you minimize taxes on the increases in the value of your assets in the future? Getting answers to these questions will put you firmly in control of your personal financial affairs.

CHAPTER 18

Accumulation in a Volatile Environment

IN A VOLATILE INVESTMENT CLIMATE, financial recovery is about what you keep. To manage your purchasing power, you need to eliminate the obstacles that stand between you and your future disposable income. Low and unpredictable returns on your investments are one of them. Increasingly, so is your tax burden.

Every accumulation strategy that aims to build future purchasing power must take personal taxation into account. But this is particularly so in a global financial crisis; economic growth, as measured by gross domestic product (GDP), is slow if not non-existent, shrinking governments' revenues from taxation and limiting the cash governments have available to pay for social services for their citizens.

Stated another way, the biggest, single source of revenue for the federal government in Canada is personal income taxation. But those revenues are declining. Taken together with government's growing need to fund Old Age Security, pensions of government employees, and transfer payments to the provinces (which must deal with the increasing health-care requirements of a large and aging population), raising more revenue will become critical. The alternative is more debt.

Governments, however, are already awash in debt. Like individuals, governments that operate in the red pay interest, and if interest rates rise in the future and governments are unable to repay their debts, default is possible. A few short years ago, such a scenario would have been highly improbable; however, recent global events have exposed the reality of fiscal instability, even at a government level.

In Canada, our federal debt-repayment plan has been pushed further into the future in anticipation of a continued global economic crisis. It is possible that this recent period of declining income tax rates may be one of the lowest for some time to come. Should governments need to raise more money quickly, the direct route is through increased taxation.

This is all the more serious should interest rates rise in the future. Governments, too, have operated within a low interest-rate environment. Should interest rates rise, the cost of servicing their massive debts will rise. Governments will have less money available to pay for much-needed social services. The results of potential tax erosion could vary but the obstacles to individual wealth creation are obvious: higher prices by way of direct taxation and user fees, and more gaps in services, which must be covered by the wealth of individuals.

To accumulate savings in such a world, tax efficiency becomes an increasingly important investment strategy. When income is taxed before you receive it, you will have less for your own consumption and savings. In addition, when governments raise "hidden" taxes, as they did in the 1980s and 1990s, purchasing power is eroded.

What do we mean by "hidden taxes"? Two examples illustrate:

1. When personal amounts and tax brackets are not fully indexed to inflation, you pay taxes on inflation-eroded dollars.
2. When governments raise the inclusion rate for the purposes of taxing capital gains (as they did in the late 1980s when the rate rose to 66⅔% and finally to 75% from 50%), investors lose twice: first because they invested expecting a lower income inclusion rate; second, because the cost base of the assets acquired is not indexed to inflation.

One of the best ways to hedge against unknown future taxation is to split income amongst family members; however, there are strict rules to follow and you would be wise to discuss "attribution rules" with your tax advisor. In addition, if possible, income-producing assets should be owned by each family member, not just one. These two strategies will help you strengthen the outputs from your investments.

Families who arm themselves with a few basics can develop a powerful tax-efficient, wealth-management strategy. Discuss the following with your professional advisors:

- Every individual has a "tax-free zone." This is the Basic Personal Amount, which, federally, was slightly more than $10,500 for the

2011 taxation year; provincially the amounts vary. The goal is to earn income up to the Basic Personal Amount in each family member's hands. Four family members, for example, each making $10,500 will pay less than one person making $42,000. In fact, the family members quite likely won't pay taxes at all. Ask your advisors how you can better maximize this opportunity.

- Our tax system is "progressive," meaning the more money you earn, the more taxes you will pay on your next dollar of earnings. As a result, the tax system is based on a series of incremental income ranges or tax brackets which determine the amount of income taxes you pay. How can your investment strategy help you average individual incomes down, while you average family income upward?

- Different income sources attract different marginal tax rates. For example, the highest marginal rates will apply to your next dollar of ordinary employment income, interest income, as well as public and private pension income, such as the Canada Pension Plan or withdrawals from your Registered Retirement Income Fund (RRIF). You should ask you advisors if family income sources can be correlated for better after-tax results.

  For example, adding new and diversified income sources, such as dividend income and capital gains income resulting from the disposition of capital assets which have increased in value, attract preferred marginal tax rates, because of the way taxes are calculated on these sources. How can each family member structure his or her savings to accumulate the most, but at the same time minimize risk in a volatile economic climate?

When you ask these questions of your financial professionals and work toward the answers for the family unit as a whole, you have accomplished an amazing feat: you have built a defensive line against the financial storm.

Focus on Taxes

Small changes in the structure of your income can, in fact, produce a significant increase in your return on investment — thanks to tax savings — which can be the difference between financial success and financial failure in times of volatility. The money you earn both actively and passively will go farther if you and your family members focus on tax efficiency.

Remember:

- **Taxes are your single greatest lifetime expense.** The less taxes you pay as a family, the more money you have to save, grow, then transition into your future. One of your immediate challenges in financial recovery is to discover how to recover from overtaxation.

- **Taxes could increase in the future.** Given our slow pace of economic growth, our declining tax base and government's growing requirement for revenues to meet demographic challenges, higher taxes are quite likely in our future. A good disaster recovery plan includes adjusting family earnings and savings decisions to accommodate higher taxes.

- **Income could be interrupted.** If the global economy continues to grow at a below-average pace, jobs may be lost as businesses retrench. Will your job be one of them? In some families, reduced hours, layoffs or termination will mean dropping from two incomes to one, and in others, it may mean a shift from full-time employment to one or more part-time incomes. In that situation, how do you stick to your savings goals? For retirees, on the other hand, the on-going financial malaise will bring continued low or unpredictable investment returns, at a time when they need to count on their accumulated capital to fund needs and wants. In both cases, an eye to tax efficiency can bridge difficult times.

- **Income sources may change.** Because of life-cycle events and economic realities, many individuals, but particularly baby boomers, are changing their retirement plans. They may be working longer, past their target retirement age. Or, they may be shifting to self-employment from employment income and supplementing their income with pension withdrawals. That will affect their personal taxation as well. However, in general, a diversity of income sources often has the positive effect of averaging down taxes over time. In addition, new actively earned income will preserve and bolster capital needed for the future.

- **Inflation is a threat, too.** How do you adjust for wage or investment return stagnation when the cost of living rises? When things cost more, using up more of your money, it will be significantly more difficult to identify saving opportunities because "redundant" income will shrink. Again, minimizing the taxes you pay on income and the disposition of your income-producing assets will hedge against inflation erosion.

In short, to accumulate more wealth in an economic environment that is expected to produce few investment returns in the foreseeable future, structure a "tax-efficient *family income*." To do so, review individual results first, then revisit those results to achieve the best outcome for the family unit.

What Can You Do to Recover?

Begin with an assessment of current income and taxes. Each individual in the family should consider the following:

- What type of income are you receiving? Are you receiving more "ordinary income" from employment or pensions, or is your income composed of dividends from small business corporations, public company dividends or capital gains income? Can you arrange your income mix to get a better tax result?
- Where is your taxable income in relation to the next tax bracket? How much additional income can you draw from that source before your income tax rate changes?
- In which tax bracket are other family members? If your spouse is taxed at a lower tax rate today or will be in the future, family income splitting may make sense. However, beware the "Attribution Rules" which apply to the shifting of income and capital to spouses and minor children. Although these rules generally prohibit the transfer of income or capital from a higher earner in the family to a lower earner, there are certain exceptions. For example, a bona fide loan — with commercial terms and prescribed interest rates — can be drawn up between spouses to transfer capital to the lower earner. In other cases, one spouse can hire the other to earn income from the family business. The tax advantages can be significant.
- What income source should be earned next? If you were to receive another source of income, what would be the tax impact? Is it possible to shift that income to another member of the family so as to minimize taxes? These are very important questions when you are discussing cash-flow requirements.

CHAPTER 19

The Ideal
"Order of Investing"

IS THERE AN IDEAL ORDER of investing? Definitely — it's one that takes into account tax efficiency as well as timing and cost. That means the accounts in which you grow your wealth are prioritized, and the length of time you keep money invested in those accounts and what it costs you to do so are given due consideration.

Remember: all investment choices are affected by taxes in one or more ways. That's an important consideration in structuring your ideal investment order. Consider the attributes of the following investment options:

- **Registered accounts.** Investments are made with either before-tax dollars or after-tax dollars. If a dollar goes into a registered account before income taxes are deducted, it obviously takes fewer dollars to meet the same objective than if you used after-tax dollars. That makes an investment in a Registered Retirement Savings Plan (RRSP), for those who have qualifying earned income, a lucrative investment.

- **Non-registered accounts.** You can structure outputs from your non-registered accounts to be tax-free (return of capital), taxed annually, or deferred and taxed in the future. It depends on which investments you select to put in your non-registered account. It's important not only to diversify sources but also to defer taxes as far into the future as possible so you can maximize growth.

- **Tax-preferred dispositions.** Upon disposition, income-producing assets may be subject to taxes in whole (this is the case of an investment in your registered account), in part (in the case of non-registered accounts) or not at all (as in the case of your Tax-Free Savings Account or the sale of your principal residence).

Tax-exempt investments, of course, are preferable but may have limitations. However, investments made with whole dollars, before taxation, accumulate faster. That makes them a superior vehicle in volatile economic times — provided investors meet the guidelines to qualify. For example, to put money into a RRSP you must have prior years' "earned income" and must be seventy-one year of age or less.

The following Family Investing Checklist can help you establish principles and set priorities for your family's investing:

- **Invest qualifying income:** If there is qualifying earned income, first maximize contributions to a RRSP and/or your employer-sponsored Registered Pension Plan (RPP) to create tax savings and new capital.
- **Leverage tax refunds:** Leverage the tax refund each member of the family receives from these investments to top up RRSP/RPP contributions for next year and/or to contribute to a TFSA.
- **Government benefits:** If you have young children or grandchildren, take advantage of Canada Education Savings Grants (CESGs) and Bonds, to fund their post-secondary education. Also, try to invest the Child Tax Benefit or Universal Child Care Benefit in a separate account for your children; that way you can legitimately report resulting investment income from these accounts in their hands. If there is a disabled person in the family, plug into the Canada Disability Savings Grants (CDSGs) and Bonds to provide pensions for that vulnerable person in the future.
- **First savings or parking money?** If you have family members who are over the age of eighteen, open TFSA accounts and contribute. It's a no brainer!
- **TFSA or RRSP? Mortgage or RRSP?** Which comes first? Basic principles of tax-efficient investing provide that pre-tax dollars grow faster. Furthermore, investment income earned in registered plans is tax-deferred, and so will grow bigger than after-tax dollars. This puts the RRSP first, unless you don't have qualifying earned income or are ineligible because of your age.

Reassessing portfolio construction. To overcome poor past performance and begin growing both income and capital again, take a close look at portfolio construction for the family as a whole. Discuss the following questions with your advisory team so, together, you can direct money into the appropriate accounts, in the proper priority for each family member:

1. Are you or your family members eligible to contribute to a RPP or RRSP?
2. Are you eligible to contribute to a TFSA?
3. Which investment products should you select for your registered account to achieve tax-efficient growth targets? What products work best in your non-registered account?
4. At what point will you have too much money in one or the other of these accounts?
5. What are the tax implications when the time comes to withdraw that money?
6. When will the income be needed? Which investment fits the length of time you expect the money to be invested? How and when will the withdrawal of your capital be taxed?
7. What is your target rate of return? How can this be more closely linked to your risk tolerance, then enhanced by tax efficiency?
8. How much risk should you take to get that target return, that is, what is the right balance between growth and preservation?
9. How will capital accumulations in each of these accounts contribute to sustainable net worth? When should those assets be transferred to your heirs?
10. Who will receive the assets upon death or disability, and what are the tax consequences? Should transfers be made during your lifetime for better results?

These questions can help you save income-producing capital within a RealWealth Management framework by choosing investments that meet four criteria: accumulation, growth, preservation and tax-efficient transitions.

Targeting Results: Accumulate, Grow, Preserve, Transition Wealth

Life and financial triggers	Strategy #1	Strategy #2
Cash-flow planning: Should you spend or save? Can you receive more from government sources?	**Accumulate:** To what tax and social benefits are you entitled? Can you use an RRSP to reduce family net income?	**Preserve:** Create purchasing power in the future by minimizing investment fees and the cost of consumer debt. Repay debt from your TFSA investment.
Tax planning: Accumulate more by investing on a family basis.	**Grow:** Review marginal tax rates for spouses and each member of the family; then develop a family investment strategy focused on splitting income.	**Preserve:** Plan to average down future taxes on accrued values of income-producing assets by ensuring assets are held by several family members.
Investment planning: Plan tax-deferred growth: maximize your "order of investing" by topping up contributions to registered accounts.	**Invest and grow in order:** • **Pre-tax:** RRSP • **Tax exempt:** TFSA, principal residence, certain types of insurance • **Non-registered:** interest, dividends, rents, royalties • **Non-financial assets:** how investments in real estate, business and other personal assets fit into the development and growth of family net worth.	**Preserve:** Discuss tax strategies to determine: • how to increase net capital gains on disposition of income-producing assets, • how tax refunds are reinvested, • how social benefits such as the Canada Child Tax Benefit can be increased and saved, • how Old Age Security clawbacks can be avoided. • how transferred assets, gifts, and inheritances should be invested.
Education planning: Plan tax-deferred growth.	**Grow:** Tap into free money. Invest in RESPs to generate Canada Education Savings Grants and Bonds.	**Grow more:** Make RRSP contribution and use refund to top up RESP.

Life and financial triggers	Strategy #1	Strategy #2
Residence planning: Preserve tax-exempt capital.	**Preserve**: Minimize non-deductible interest and fees: reduce amortization period, term of loan and loan rate.	**Grow:** Make RRSP contributions and the pay off mortgage with your refunds. Withdraw money tax-free from an RRSP under the Home Buyers' Plan to fund a first-time home purchase. Discuss insurance strategies to protect family assets in the case of death or disability.
Retirement planning: Preserve capital and pension pools tax efficiently.	**Accumulate:** Invest more of the first dollar earned; invest it the longest, then keep more by averaging down the taxes you pay on your withdrawals. That means your withdrawal strategy should be part of your accumulation strategy. When will you start to withdraw and generate tax? What will you do with redundant income at that time? Continue to accumulate by minimizing tax withholdings and quarterly tax instalments.	**Preserve:** Save as much as you can in an RRSP, make spousal RRSP contributions to split future retirement income; reinvest refunds, then plan "melt-down" strategies that minimize capital encroachment. This will allow you to continue to accumulate — possibly in a more advantageous investment climate in the future — while meeting your basic needs.
Estate planning: Preserve income and capital for the next generation.	**Grow:** Discuss the transfer of assets during your lifetime and at death, to grow assets in the right hands; minimize risk with insurance strategies for long-term financial security.	**Preserve what you have built:** Discuss the amount of taxes to be paid on death, then structure wills, buy-sell agreements, charitable giving and ongoing loss applications so as to minimize taxes in the estate.

Transition With Purchasing Power

The most significant financial moment in life is the moment before you die. That is when your final net worth is calculated and the transfer of asset to your heirs begins.

At that time, all your assets are given a "fair market" value. Your estate will pay taxes on the difference between the fair market value and the price at which you acquired the assets, or the "adjusted cost base." An exception is when your spouse survives you. In that case, there is a "tax-free rollover."

Of course, with the aid of an astute tax practitioner, your estate may be able to establish a value between the assets' cost base and fair market value by bumping up the cost base without necessarily adding costs, particularly if the deceased had unused capital losses, large medical expenses or charitable donations. That's an important strategy if you want to save tax dollars when the surviving spouse dies.

By understanding how the fair market value and adjusted cost base applies to your family assets, you'll be in a better position to determine when to transfer those assets — during your lifetime or at death — and to whom. You'll also understand how to utilize capital losses better.

This is also a good time to understand the role insurance can play in transition planning. The right insurance coverage will pay income taxes at your death and shore up any losses you may have experienced in your portfolio. Your insurance specialist, in collaboration with your tax advisor, will help you make the appropriate decisions for your time and money.

When this is done well, your financial legacy is transferred as intact as possible to your heirs. That's an important part of your family's financial recovery from the effects of the financial crisis.

What Can You Do to Recover?

- Work with your professional advisor team to establish your ideal order of investing.
- Take the timing of withdrawals, the tax implications and the costs of investing into account.
- Remember the importance of minimizing the taxes you pay, in order to grow your wealth faster.

CHAPTER 20

Maintaining Financial Dignity

THE TRULY WEALTHY are principled builders who enjoy peace of mind. They meet basic needs, then purposefully use their resources of time and money to invest for tomorrow according to a plan that sets milestones for financial results.

Most important, they understand that possessing an abundance of money requires a *business approach*, not an emotional approach. A business approach employs strategy and process, as well as a great team of people, and executes according to a well-defined plan.

Those who build Real Wealth — with sustainability and purchasing power — generally have common characteristics. You may recognize these or aspire to them, but in any case, they are good rules for getting you through a financial crisis:

1. **They live modestly.** Despite their income, they live a modest lifestyle. This maximizes the amount of money left over to invest in wealth-building activities, no matter how difficult the economic climate.

2. **They avoid waste.** They consider it morally wrong to waste time or money. Given that rule, they use their time wisely, avoid wasteful spending and treat their money as an income-producing tool.

3. **They save aggressively.** Thomas Stanley and William Danko, the authors of *The Millionaire Next Door*,[1] found that the typical person

---

[1] Thomas J. Stanley and Willam Danko, *The Millionaire Next Door: the Surprising Secrets of America's Wealthy* (Marietta, Ga.: Longstreet Press, 1996).

of wealth is a very aggressive saver. This individual invests 15% to 20% — or more — of his or her income each year in assets that grow in value. This allocation does not include the principal residence, which is a significant contributor to family wealth.

4. **They have a plan for their money and they follow it.**

5. **They control debt.** They don't spend money they don't have. If they use credit, it is within a business context, and/or the credit is backed by assets they own.

6. **They understand their tax burden and how it can erode their wealth.** They structure their affairs within the framework of the law to pay the least possible taxes on an individual and a family basis, minimizing taxes on both income and capital.

7. **They understand the time value of money.** They have a sense of urgency about investing for the future today, so as to maximize long-term growth. They recognize that the longer they put off building wealth, the smaller the benefit of compounding returns over the long term. They also understand that the opposite is true for long-term debts such as mortgages.

8. **They think on an intergenerational basis.** They want to make sure their efforts benefit future generations. As they plan their affairs, they focus on strategies that will preserve wealth from taxes, death and divorce, at the same time preparing others to be stewards of the wealth that will be transitioned to them.

9. **They protect what they have.** They recognize how hard it is and how long it takes to build up wealth with so many external obstacles to overcome; they also know how easily and quickly wealth can disappear. Therefore, as time goes on and the level of overall wealth climbs, they are often increasingly focused on preservation.

10. **They use the services of professional advisors to their advantage.** They seek to make decisions jointly with their advisors to achieve a state of affluence:
    - **Independence**, resulting from the use of financial *skills*,
    - **Peace of mind**, resulting from use of financial *knowledge*,
    - **Confident and purposeful decision-making**, *behavior* which enables individuals to live and retire in dignity, with enough resources to cover both needs and wants, while they preserve their wealth.

Financial recovery in a fragile world is possible. It may be painful and your convalescence may be slow, but with a sound framework within which to think through important financial decisions, that recovery can be accelerated, positioning you for a golden future.

You, too, can live with financial dignity, especially if you resolve to react to a changing financial world with a purposeful framework designed to give you and your family peace of mind.

What Can You Do to Recover?

- Have a multi-generational Real Wealth Management strategy, the directional document for all advisors on the professional advisory team. It links financial activities to four elements: accumulation, growth, preservation and transition of sustainable family wealth with purchasing power, that is, after taxes, inflation and fees.
- Develop a list of key stakeholders that includes your key advisors and their roles in the overall process, as well as all family members involved in building a powerful economic unit that will fortify your wealth against the volatility in the global economy.
- Revisit your vision, principles and benchmarks often, based on your key financial triggers and objectives. Financial recovery is a continuum: as you and your world change, so, too, must the use of your money adapt and change.
- Work with the numbers. Evaluate your personal and family net worth statements, to ensure you are financially stable and that your net worth is meeting growth targets.
- Update your financial plan so you can plan ahead and save for various life events. Each component of your financial plan, and the accompanying investment product selections, should help you achieve your accumulation, growth and preservation goals. Your plan should include a summary of your objectives, analysis, calculations and recommendations, and should be reviewed periodically and adjusted to present circumstances. Your plan helps you execute on your overall wealth-management plan and prevents you from make reactive responses to a volatile marketplace.
- Keep a keen eye on taxes, inflation and the ongoing costs of using your money because they can erode your wealth. When you minimize these costs your financial health increases.
- To achieve your ideal state of affluence, focus on protecting your family assets now and on an inter-generational basis.

PART 4

Our Fragile World

CHAPTER 21

Lessons Learned

WE HAVE COME A LONG WAY since that day in September 2008, when a bankruptcy in New York shook the foundations of the Western world. The economic meltdown that followed not only sent governments and businesses reeling but also dug deep into the pocket books of regular people. In the intervening years, some people have lost their houses, some have lost their jobs, still others have abandoned their plans for a rosy retirement and many have relinquished their dreams of passing on wealth to the next generation.

But we are on the road to financial recovery, even if it is a long and bumpy road. And although our destination is still some distance off, there is reason for cautious optimism.

If there is any thing we have learned since 2008, it is the role debt has played in causing the turbulence of recent years. Many developed countries have a debt-to-GDP ratio that is well in excess of 85%, the point at which, researchers tell us, debt becomes a drag on economic growth.[1]

Best estimates put Japan's debt-to-GDP ratio at 228% in 2011; Greece's ratio was 167% while in the United States, debt-to-GDP was nudging 100%. In Canada, we have a toe on the line at 84%. For years, it seems, governments have fueled their economic growth with debt; now they are mired in it, making it very difficult to continue spending their way out the downturn.

---

[1] Stephen G. Cecchetti, M.S. Mohanty and Fabrizio Zampolli, "The real effects of debt," *Bank for International Settlements Working Papers* No. 352 (September 2011).

Debt, in short, has tied the hands of government leaders looking for resolutions to today's malaise and, worse, has threatened government's ability to fund the services their citizens have counted on to secure their futures.

Lesson learned: the more debt you have the fewer choices you have.

It isn't just central government debt that is slowing our journey to economic recovery. It is corporate and personal debt as well. In Canada, if we add together government, corporate and personal debt-to-GDP ratios, we get 313%, well in excess of the standard of 260% established by our aforementioned researchers.[2] A number of Western countries have similar if not worse results. In the U.S., personal debt alone was US$16 trillion in 2011 — more than the country's national debt.

So, we have a triple whammy with which to contend in our collective financial recovery. Governments are awash in debt and any attempts to spend their way out of the downturn will only worsen the situation. Frightened individuals — worried about jobs, shrinking asset values and rising personal debt — are pulling in their horns. Many have reduced or stopped spending, and for good reason — about thirty million people have lost their jobs globally.[3]

Sinking demand both domestically and internationally has also hurt businesses, likewise burdened with debt. In addition to sagging demand at home, the U.S. recession and global economic weakness have lowered exports and reduced manufacturing activities. Businesses have had to work even harder if they are to restore equity to balances sheets and find money to innovate. Credit and venture capital have become increasingly hard to secure. This takes its toll on revenues; as they vanish, businesses are forced to react quickly to reduce production, cut spending and lower employment.

It is a vicious circle. Government, corporate and personal debt all feed the fear and strengthen the drag on economic growth.

Lesson learned: we are in a prolonged period of sluggish growth.

The result of a prolonged economic slowdown is that financially strapped governments lose even more revenue from anticipated tax receipts. They delay debt management and deficit reduction.

---

[2] Ibid.
[3] Bank of Canada statistics, 17 November 2011.

Sluggish growth also scares already-spooked individuals but, in particular, baby boomers. The leading edge of the baby boom generation is hitting sixty-five and many are delaying retirement because the financial crisis has devastated their savings.

Yet, the outlook is not grim. We may, in fact, be moving from critical to stable condition. If recognizing the problem is the first step, then we are on the road to financial recovery. Eurozone trouble spots Greece and Italy have brought in new governments to steer those countries through a period of refinancing. The U.S., despite the staggering loss of wealth since 2007, is in a period of subdued growth. The International Monetary Fund (IMF), in its October 2011 Western Hemisphere report, put 2011 growth at 1.5% and 2012 growth at 1.8%.[4] The wild card is the political situation leading into the 2012 election. But, perhaps, we can take some encouragement from the bickering of U.S. politicians, in that, at least, they have grasped how serious the problem is.

In Canada, we are living with the effects of weaker U.S. and global growth. After growing by slightly more than 2% in 2011, the economy is projected to grow by slightly less than 2% in 2012.[5] However, labour markets have performed well and private credit remains strong. The federal government seems to have its hand firmly on the controls, anticipating a return to budget surplus by 2016. Domestic demand, though weaker than anticipated in 2011, continues to be a catalyst for growth. The IMF, however, raises one red flag: the high level of household debt and possible "retrenchment" amid concerns about falling house prices.[6]

Lessons learned: it takes time to recover from indebtedness.

If we are experiencing what respected economist Richard Koo calls a "balance sheet recession," we are simply going to have to wait until governments, businesses and households pay down debt and restore balance. Low interest rates and continued credit availability will not get them to spend until they have minimized debt. But when individuals and businesses work hard to reduce debt at the expense of spending, governments have to take up the slack and replace consumer and corporate spending with government programs. That's a difficult balancing act for governments at all levels.

---

[4] "Regional Economic Outlook: Western Hemisphere, Shifting Winds, New Policy Challenges," International Monetary Fund, October 2011, p. 4, found at: http://www.imf.org/external/pubs/ft/reo/2011/whd/eng/pdf/wreo1011.pdf, accessed 20 November 2011.
[5] Ibid., p. 7.
[6] Ibid., p. 8.

Still, governments, businesses and individuals everywhere are beginning to get their financial houses in order. Canadians should take that message to heart; we are still spending more than we have and paying for it with debt. You can't save for the future — there is no "redundant income" from which to produce income-producing capital — if you are burdened with debt. And sadly, your debt, rather than your wealth, becomes the legacy of the next generation.

Lesson learned: get your financial house in order.

If governments are to continue spending until the private sector minimizes debt, they have few places to go for additional funds. Governments' biggest source of revenue is taxes on income. There are two ways to boost those revenues: one is by growing the economy, which is not too likely in our post-2008 world. The other is by raising taxes. That is a likely scenario in the coming years and that puts all the more emphasis on handling your personal finances in a tax-savvy way.

So, minimize personal income taxes; know your marginal tax rate. Take a family approach and employ income splitting; diversify your sources of income so you pay less. And don't forget the ideal order of investing. The steps you can take are many if you want to build real wealth.

Lesson learned: Don't pay unnecessary taxes on income; invest capital tax-efficiently.

Perhaps the most important thing you can do to enhance your financial recovery in a fragile world is work with a professional advisory team — your lawyer, tax accountant, financial advisors, estate planning specialist — with the most trusted of your advisors being your Real Wealth Manager.

The goal of a Real Wealth Management Plan is sustainable family wealth, regardless of the economic cycle. This strategic framework takes an integrated approach to the accumulation, growth, preservation and transition of sustainable family wealth, but with purchasing power now and in the future. That puts a strong emphasis on managing the eroding effect of inflation and taxes. But, to do that well, you will want to work not only with your professional advisory team but also with your family members. Together, the decisions you make will take you closer to your Real Wealth goals.

If you are to survive and thrive in a fragile world, you have to manage those aspects of your financial well-being that you can control — such as the amount of debt in your balance sheet, the amount you spend and the amount you save, choosing the right advisors and following their advice, and making decisions jointly with your family and advisors so you are always moving toward your goals.

To do that well — and avoid reactive and emotional responses to a volatile marketplace — you need to understand, monitor and evaluate the changes in your personal net worth statement, your tax returns and your financial plan. Do that and you will make wiser choices on how you build a tax-efficient investment portfolio.

Lesson learned: you can't control global economic changes and government policies but you can put your household's financial recovery on a sound footing with a strategic plan designed just for you.

What Can You Do to Recover?

- Lower debt: the more debt you have the fewer choices you have.
- Expect a prolonged period of sluggish growth and have realistic expectations about the performance of your investment portfolio.
- Get your financial house in order. You won't be able to accumulate and preserve income-producing capital if you are not financially stable.
- Don't pay unnecessary taxes on income; invest tax-efficiently.
- Plan to pay the least amount of taxes on your accrued capital gains with the right asset transfer plan during your lifetime and at death.
- You can't control government policy so take control where you can. Build your professional advisory team, engage your family and make decisions that result in sustainable family wealth with purchasing power, over multiple generations.

Bibliography

Agathe, C., Jocelyn Jacob, John Nelmes & Miles Whittingham, "Inflation Expectations and Real Return Bonds," *Bank of Canada Review* Summer 1996: pp. 41-53.

Alessi, Christopher. "The Eurozone In Crisis." *Council on Foreign Relations* 18 October 2011.

Alexander, Craig. "Paying the Piper." TD Bank Group [Toronto], 28 September 2011.

"Baby Boomers." Spectrem Group: Chicago, March 2011.

Bak, Per. *How Nature Works: The Science of Self-Organized Criticality.* New York: Copernicus, 1996.

"Bank Failures in Brief." Federal Deposit Insurance Corporation. www.fdic.gov/bank/historical/bank/2008/index.html

"Banking in the United States," *Encyclopedia Americana* (Grolier online).

"Bankrupt Canada?" *Wall Street Journal* 12 January1995: page A14.

Barber, Brad M., Yn-Tsung Lee, Yu-Jane Liu and Terrance Odean, "Just How Much Do Individual Investors Lose by Trading?" *Review of Financial Studies*, vol. 22, no.2 (2009), pp.609-632.

Brückner, Markus and Anita Tuladhar. "Public Investment as a Fiscal Stimulus: Evidence from Japan's Regional Spending During the 1990s." International Monetary Fund *Working Paper* April 2010.

Buchanan, Mark. *Ubiquity: Why Catastrophes Happen.* New York: Three Rivers Press, 2002.

Cameron, Fraser. "The European Union as a Model for Regional Integration." *Council on Foreign Relations* September 2010.

Canadian Federal Budget Papers 27 January 2009.

Cecchetti, Stephen G., M.S. Mohanty and Fabrizio Zampolli. "The real effects of debt." *Bank for International Settlements Working Papers* No. 352, September 2011.

Clinton, Kevin. "The Term Structure of Interest Rates as a Leading Economic Indicator: A Technical Note." *Bank of Canada Review* Winter 1994-1995.

Colander, David and Michael Goldberg, Armin Haas, Katarina Juselius, Alan Kirman, Thomas Lux and Brigitte Sloth. "The Financial Crisis and the Systemic Failure of the Economics Profession." *Critical Review* 21, nos. 2-3, 2009.

Davies, James. "Efficiency and Effectiveness of Savings Instruments Design." Research Working Group on Retirement Income Adequacy, Department of Finance Canada, 3 December 2009.

"Dr. Keynes's Chinese Patient." *The Economist* [London] 13 November 2008.

Elements of Real Wealth Management Certificate Course. Winnipeg: Knowledge Bureau, 2011.

Feldstein, Martin. "Japan's Saving Crisis," Project Syndicate, 24 September 2010.

Ganzel, Bill. "Farming in the 1930s." *Wessels Living History Farm* [York, Nebraska] 2003.

Global Competitiveness Report 2011-2012. World Economic Forum. Geneva, 2011.

Gordon, Stephen. Mainly Canadian Economic Blog. http://worthwhile.typepad. com/worthwhile_canadian_initi/2011/06/balance-sheet.html#more 21 June 2011.

Government at a Glance 2011. Paris: Organization for Economic Cooperation and Development, 2011.

"Historical Statistics for Banking." Federal Deposit Insurance Corporation.

"How will Japan pay for reconstruction." *The Economist* 14 March 2011.

Jacks, Evelyn. *Essential Tax Facts.* Winnipeg: Knowledge Bureau, 2011.

Jisi, Wang. "China's Search for a Grand Strategy: A Rising Great Power Finds Its Way." *Foreign Affairs Magazine* March/April 2011.

Kim, Seoyoung, April Klein and James Rosenfeld, "Return Performance Surrounding Reverse Stock Splits: Can Investors Profit?" *Financial Management* 37 issue 2, Summer, 200: pp. 173-192.

Koo, Richard. "America lacks the necessary commitment to stimulus." *The Economist* 26 July 2010.

Kotlikoff, Laurence. "U.S. is bankrupt and we don't even know it." *Bloomberg* 10 August 2010.

Krudy, Edward. "Volatility stymies even smart money." *Reuters* 16 September 2011.

Macklem, Tiff. "Managing Risks in the New Economic Landscape." 27 September 2011.

Maddison, Angus. *Contours of the World Economy, 1–2003 AD: Essays in Macroeconomic History.* New York: Oxford University Press, 2007.

Manolopoulos, Jason. *Greece's Odious Debt: The Looting of the Hellenic Republic by the Euro, the Political Elite and the Investment Community.* London: Anthem Press, 2011.

Maymin, Philip Z. and Gregg S. Fisher. "Preventing Emotional Investing: An Added Value of an Investment Advisor." *Journal of Wealth Management* Spring 2011.

Miller, Geoffrey P. "The Role of a Central Bank in a Bubble Economy." *Cardozo Law Review,* Vol. 18, No 3, December 1996.

Mintz, Jack M. *Summary Report on Retirement Income Adequacy Research.* Department of Finance Canada, 18 December 2009.

Nelson, Douglas. *Master Your Retirement: How to fulfill your dreams with peace of mind.* Winnipeg: Knowledge Bureau, 2012.

Pigeon, Marc-Andre. "The Debt-to-GDP Target: Options and Considerations." Parliamentary Information and Research Service, 11 May 2005.

"Regional Economic Outlook: Western Hemisphere, Shifting Winds, New Policy Challenges," International Monetary Fund, October 2011.

Rhodes, David and Daniel Stelter, *Stop Kicking the Can Down the Road: The price of not addressing the root causes of the crisis.* Boston Consulting Group, August 2011.

Rose, Andrew K. and Mark M. Spiegel. "Cross-Country Causes and Consequences of the 2008 Crisis: Early Warning." *FRBSF Working Paper* 2009-17.

Rose, Andrew K. and Mark M. Spiegel. " Predicting Crises, Part II: Did Anything Matter (to Everybody)?" *FRBSF Economic Letters* 28 September 2009.

Siegel, Jeremy. *Stocks for the Long Run.* New York, McGraw Hill, 1994.

Siegel, Jeremy. *The Future for Investors: Why the Tried and the True Triumph Over the Bold and the New.* New York: Crown Business, 2005.

"Sovereign default in the Eurozone: Greece and Beyond." UBS Wealth Management Research, October 2011.

Stanley, Thomas J. and Willam Danko. *The Millionaire Next Door: the Surprising Secrets of America's Wealthy.* Marietta, Ga.: Longstreet Press, 1996.

Taleb, Nassim Nicholas. *The Black Swan: The Impact of the Highly Improbable.* New York: Random House, 2007.

"The Wealth of Canadians." Statistics Canada, 2006.

Thornton, Mark. "The Japanese Bubble Economy." www.lewrockwell.com 23 May 2004.

Turchansky, Ray. "Debt-ceiling deal in US has investors pondering their next moves," *Post Media News* 13 August 2011.

Watson, William. "As Triple A as we Think." *National Post* 9 September 2011: p. FP11

Young, Lauren. "Is Citigroup's Reverse Stock Split a Smart Move?" *Bloomberg Businessweek* 19 March 2009.

Resources

Bank of Canada. www.bankofcanada.ca

BMO Financial Group. www.bmo.com

Board of Governors of the Federal Reserve System. www.federalreserve.gov

Canada Department of Finance. www.fin.gc.ca

Council of Europe. www.coe.int/lportal/web/coe-portal

Federal Deposit Insurance Corporation. www2.fdic.gov/hsob/index.asp and www.fdic.gov

Financial Crisis Inquiry Report. Final Report of the National Commission on the Causes of the Financial and Economic Crisis in the United States. January 2011 http://cybercemetery.unt.edu/archive/fcic/20110310173738/http://www.fcic.gov/report/

Financial Planning Standards Council. www.fpsc.ca

Jeremy Siegel. www.jeremysiegel.com.

Knowledge Bureau. www.knowledgebureau.com

MeasuringWorth. www.MeasuringWorth.com

Moneychimp. www.moneychimp.com

Nasdaq Stock Market. www.nasdaq.com

Office of the Superintendent of Financial Institutions. www.osfi-bsif.gc.ca

Organization for Economic Cooperation and Development. http://stats.oecd.org

Quotations Page. www.quotationspage.com

Royal Bank of Canada. www.rbc.com

Statistics Canada. www.statcan.gc.ca

U.S. Department of Commerce, Bureau of Economic Analysis. www.bea.gov

U.S. Department of the Treasury. www.treasury.gov/Pages/default.aspx

U.S. National Debt Clock. www.usdebtclock.org.

Wikipedia. http://en.wikipedia.org

World Bank. http://data.worldbank.org

Yahoo Finance. http://ca.finance.yahoo.com.

Index